GUNPOWDER TREASON AND PLOT

C. Northcote Parkinson

There is only one event in Britain's history which is given annual remembrance – the discovery of the Gunpowder Plot in 1605. With the ritual burning of Guy Fawkes surrounded by an exploding array of fireworks, the salvation of King James I from the hands of the assassin is celebrated each November 5th. Behind this popular myth lies a story of political intrigue and religious conflict, comparable to a modern thriller, and attempts to establish what actually happened have caused heated controversy for centuries.

C. Northcote Parkinson's interest in the Gunpowder Plot derives from the fact that he and Guy Fawkes attended the same school – St Peter's, one of the oldest schools in England, the royal and cathedral school of York. Earlier historians have tended to adopt one of two opposite points of view. Protestants have accepted the official story, agreeing that militant catholics planned to murder the King in Parliament. Some catholic apologists, on the other hand, have denied the reality of the plot or questioned, at least, whether its existence has ever been proved. They have pointed to contradictions in the evidence and cast doubts on the value of testimony extracted by torture. Some scholars have suggested that the plot was devised by the Earl of Salisbury and certain it is that no conspiracy could have better

Parkinson presents with absorbing and enlightening detail, serves to remind us of the bomb scares of an earlier age.

Gunpowder,
Treason and Plot

Gunpowder, Treason and Plot

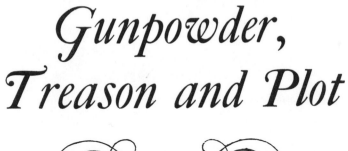

C. NORTHCOTE PARKINSON

St. Martin's Press New York

Contents

List of Illustrations

Elizabeth's England

THE United Kingdom, as we know it today, was formed for the purpose of external conquest. The unification was, in fact, the essential preliminary to the campaigns which were to establish the British Empire. The loosening of that unity today is the logical consequence of that empire's collapse; such a unity being no longer essential or even convenient. In 1600, however, the effective conquest of Ireland, just begun, was about to be followed by the merger with Scotland; and William Shakespeare, for one, knew exactly what was happening, and why. England, in the meanwhile, was small in itself as compared with France or Spain. It may have had some three and a half or even four million people. For practical purposes the bulk of this population was of no importance. Many of the heads counted were those of illiterate peasants in remote counties, anxious only that government would leave them alone. Those living in London had rather more influence and these may have numbered a quarter of a million.

In 1605 ... Creighton suggests a population of 224,275 (about 76,000 for the City, 113,000 for the Liberties and outer wards, 36,000 for the out-parishes). In addition we should probably have to reckon between 20,000 and 30,000 for Westminster, Stepney, Lambeth etc. This makes a total population for Greater London of 250,000. If this is correct the Venetian Ambassador's suggestion that the population in 1606 was 300,000 is too high, but not so absurd as was once thought.[1]

Of the total population in London and other cities, the influential minority was quite small and in the countryside the population was smaller still, the gentry being mostly known and indeed related to each other and known again to government. In studying Jacobean history our concern is more with individuals and families than with people in the mass. In any given county the folk of consequence would be relatively few. The population, of high and low degree, was divided in religion but in proportions now impossible to determine. Henry VIII lived and died a Catholic but opened the way to a Protestant ascendancy under his youthful successor. The early death of Edward VI led, in turn, to a Catholic revival under Mary Tudor with a persecution now of the Protestants. She was succeeded in 1558 by Queen Elizabeth I, who inaugurated a persecution of the Catholics which was to last, with varying intensity, for the whole of her reign. She was destined to die unmarried and childless and she was to be succeeded, as we know, by another Protestant monarch, but there was nothing inevitable about this at the time. For all the loyal subject could tell, Elizabeth might be succeeded by a Catholic and he/she again by a Protestant, with each party being persecuted in its turn. To prevent this alternation became a main object of policy; one more cherished, naturally, by the party in power but essential, in fact, to everyone. But what is obvious now was not so apparent then. The Catholics under Elizabeth were mostly biding their time and they had no reason to doubt that their time would come.

How many Catholics were there? We have no means of knowing nor of deciding even, what definition of the word we should accept. They fell, in truth, into a number of indistinct categories. There were the fanatically religious, ready to fight or die for their faith and eager, in the meanwhile, to recruit others who would be as militant. There were the deeply religious whose orthodoxy was not in question but who were content to lie low until Protestant rule should come to its appointed end. Then there were the Church papists who occasionally attended their Protestant place of worship as a matter of form but who went to mass in private. There were apparently devout members of a Protestant congregation who would certainly revert to Catholicism if given the chance. There were people who cared little about religion but whose preference, on balance, was for the old ways rather than the new. There were many intermediate shades of belief and many, like Elizabeth herself, who were careful to express no belief of any kind. As between the extremes of belief there were perhaps a majority of people who would follow the government in power, being not of the stuff of which martyrs are made.

Neither religious party was prepared to tolerate the other and we are apt today to blame them both for their intolerance. We might do better, however, to understand it. Their institutions were rooted in a medieval world to which the separation of powers was quite unknown. Surviving from the Middle Ages is that central institution, the papacy, the functions of which are religious, political, educational, financial, administrative, legal and diplomatic. Other medieval institutions were similarly unspecialized, the larger monasteries, for example, combining big business with piety. And while the Reformation had abolished some of this structure it left other parts unchanged. In England, for example, the Archbishop of Canterbury was (and in theory still is) one of the great officers of the Crown; a member of what we should now call the Cabinet. The Bishop of Durham was responsible for the defence of his diocese against the Scots. Every bishop had his own consistory court with a wide jurisdiction and considerable powers. Each parish was an administrative as well as a religious unit with a wide range of functions extending from police work to garbage collection. And if ostensibly religious bodies had an administrative aspect, the supposedly economic trade guilds had their religious side. The individual who professed a minority religious belief was thus held to be rejecting society as a whole, shirking his duties and refusing to pull his weight. To have more than one accepted creed within a kingdom did not at first seem even technically possible. We know that means were eventually found to isolate the executive and judicial functions and disentangle the religious from the political office. It was far from easy, however, and it was the work of successive generations. When James I argued that the abolition of the bishops would mean the abolition of the monarchy, he was saying little more than most men would have thought obvious. Church and State were but different aspects of a single society and to separate them would be to destroy the

3

whole. Toleration was a concept more or less outside the range of seventeenth-century thought.

The Protestant party had ruled England since the accession of Queen Elizabeth, but was their rule to be permanent? There was no certainty about this. Elizabeth was the last of the Tudors and her proper successor was Mary, Queen of Scots, a Catholic. There were other possible claimants but none with as good a claim as Mary, whose very name suggested a repetition of the last Marian persecution in which about three hundred people were executed. For Elizabethan politicians and above all for that central character, Lord Burghley, the whole fate of the realm depended on the life of a woman who refused to marry and produce an heir. What if she were assassinated? Such a disaster could easily happen, as was proved by the fate of William of Orange, killed by a Catholic fanatic in 1584. Her death, while Mary lived, would mean civil war. Nor was she an easy monarch to protect. She moved freely among crowds of people and rejected all special precautions to ensure her safety. Worse still, she travelled round England and was often the guest of people whose loyalty might be thought doubtful. Her travel plans were governed, indeed, by political considerations. When she suspected that any family might be plotting against her, often her plan was to pay them a visit. They could not plot whilst she was there and they were financially ruined by the time she left. To take a random example, her visit to Euston Hall in 1578 must have rendered the Rookwoods harmless for the next decade. Her policy was astute but her ministers were appalled at the risks she would run, seemingly unaware of the fact that her life (and theirs) was at stake.

Generally responsible for her safety was her Lord High Treasurer – William Cecil, Lord Burghley – who founded the secret service in 1570. This was the year in which Pope Pius v signed the papal bull *Regnans in Excelcis*, the act by which Elizabeth was finally excommunicated. This bull has been fairly described as an uncompromising document, as the following extract may serve to suggest:

... But the number of the Ungodly hath gotten such Power ... and amongst others, Elizabeth, the pretended Queen of England, the Servant of Wickedness, lendeth thereunto her helping hand, with whom, as in a Sanctuary, the most pernicious persons have found a Refuge. This very Woman, having seized on the Kingdom, and monstrously usurped the place of Supreme Head of the Church in all England, and the chief Authority and Jurisdiction thereof, hath again reduced the said Kingdom into a miserable and ruinous condition ...

We do out of the fullness of our apostolick Power, declare the aforesaid Elizabeth as being a Heretick and a Favourer of Hereticks, and her adherents in the matters aforesaid, to have incurred the Sentence of Excommunication and to be cut off from the Unity of the Body of Christ. And moreover, we do declare her to be deprived of her pretended Title to the Kingdom aforesaid, and of all Dominion, Dignity and Privilege whatsoever; and also the Nobility, Subjects and People of the said Kingdom and all the others who have in any sort sworn unto her, to be for ever absolved from any such Oath, and all manner of Duty of Dominion, Allegiance and Obedience: and we also do by authority of these Present absolve them and do deprive the said Elizabeth of her pretended title to the Kingdom and all other things before named. And we do command and charge all and every the Noblemen, Subjects, People and others aforesaid, that they presume not to obey her, or Her Orders, Mandates and Laws: and those which shall do the contrary, we do include them in the like Sentence of Anathema.[2]

Pope Pius v was a former Dominican friar, a stern theologian and moralist, and he acted on the advice of the Earls of Northumberland and Westmorland, Catholic adherents of Mary, Queen of Scots. The latter was already in exile, living at Louvain and about to be attainted and deprived of his estates. The former (Henry Percy, 8th Earl) was not arrested until the following year. The pope who accepted their suggestion had failed to consult the king of Spain, who would have advised him against doing anything so foolish. The immediate effect of the bull was to divide and confuse the English Catholics. The Church papists were forbidden, in effect, to practise their occasional conformity and were told to become recusants. They were offered a choice, in fact, of becoming openly hostile to Elizabeth or openly disobedient to the pope. To obey Elizabeth was to be excommunicated. It cannot be said that they were urged in so many words to assassinate their sovereign but the pope said nothing to discourage such an attempt. Elizabeth might fairly assume that her assassin would be given no more than a nominal penance. It was at this point

that Lord Burghley's secret agents began to go into action, antici-
pating the sort of trouble that would probably ensue. Agents at
home or abroad, however, were not answerable directly to him. They
were placed more immediately under the control of Sir Francis
Walsingham, Secretary of State from 1573 to 1590, and a member
of the Privy Council.

... there were probably never more than about a dozen full-time professional
agents on his pay-roll at any given moment. Reliable spies, always in short
supply, tended to come expensive and it was not until 1582 that Walsingham
first began to receive any sort of regular budget for this side of his work. It
started at a grudging £750 per annum and was gradually increased to £2,000
by 1588, two years before his death. In the early days most of the cost of
maintaining a secret service is said to have come from its founder's own pocket.

From the list drawn up after his death, it seems that Walsingham was in the
habit of receiving information from ... [France, Germany, Italy, Spain and
the Low Countries]. In addition to his foreign network he had four regular
agents in England, engaged in tracking the movements of the Jesuit and
seminary priests. One way and another it would probably be no exaggeration
to say that very little went on in Catholic circles either at home or abroad
during the 1580s which did not, sooner or later, come to the notice of that
'most subtle searcher of secrets', Sir Francis Walsingham.[3]

A total of four full-time agents may seem unimpressive but the men
they were tracking were also relatively few. At one period the Jesuit
priests in England are thought to have numbered seventeen; at a
later period there would seem to have been about forty. No great
statistical accuracy is to be expected but we are dealing with a silent
war in which only a handful of men were involved on either side.

Until about 1580 Elizabethan policy had been to let Catholicism
die out in England by a natural process. People brought up in the
old faith would be elderly folk, unlikely to live for very long. Surviving priests would have been ordained, at the latest, over twenty
years earlier, and without a bishop no further priests could be provided. Given time, it was thought, the problem would solve itself
without needless pressure or cruelty. And the more pessimistic
Catholics were ready to accept that situation, confident of heaven for
themselves but unable to do too much for the salvation of their

children. Other Catholics, however, sent their children for education overseas and some of them for training at Douai or some other seminary for the priesthood. As if this was not bad enough, there followed the impact of the Counter Reformation. The Jesuits came to England in 1580, headed by Robert Parsons and Edmund Campion, and began to make converts among the gentry. Campion was martyred in 1581 and Robert Parsons left England to become, eventually, rector of the English College at Rome. It was he who directed the Jesuit campaign in Elizabethan England. From the government's point of view, the Jesuits altered the whole situation. The Catholics were no longer dwindling but had actually become more numerous. There had been conversions, some in very good families, and the converts showed a new fanaticism, a new kind of missionary zeal. These were dissidents who did not acknowledge Elizabeth as their queen. Here were people fit for treason, stratagems and spoils. There was every reason, therefore, to treat these folk with the greatest severity, more especially in periods of external danger when they might well be in active league with the enemy.

While the Jesuit activities were treasonable and highly dangerous they also served to emphasize the split between the old Catholics and the new converts: a split which began in 1570 and widened afterwards. Still more helpful to Elizabeth was the fact that whereas the old Catholics had a traditional contact with France and so with Mary Stuart, the Jesuits had more contact with Spain where the Infanta was a rival candidate for the English throne. For purposes of counter-espionage, Walsingham was to make good use of this Catholic disunity. He knew all about it and had his own agent, naturally, in the English College of Rome. With England actually at war with Spain from 1587, it was easy to arouse popular feeling against the Jesuits and their 'Jesuited' supporters. As against that, the behaviour of Mary Stuart did something to discourage her potential supporters in England. There was no Catholic bishop to plead for union but the pope did appoint an 'archpriest' whose duty was to reconcile these different points of view. At the end of Elizabeth's reign the archpriest was a certain George Blackwell, who inclined rather to the Jesuit side but would not seem to have had much influence either way. One great achievement of the Jesuits had been to set up their own secret printing press and this was still active in George Blackwell's day. One way and another a minister in Walsingham's position had a great deal to do.

Francis Walsingham (1530?–1590) is not a character who comes alive in contemporary comment and description. He took up the duties of Principal Secretary in 1574 but had no very considerable secret service until 1580 and nothing very highly organized at the time of the Throckmorton Treason of 1584. Some authors have regarded Walsingham as the key figure in a police state. This is not a helpful description, as Alison Plowden points out:

> In some circles Francis Walsingham has the reputation of a sixteenth-century Lavrenti Beria. Somewhat closer inspection reveals the disappointing reality of a conscientious, over-worked and under-staffed government official, frequently in poor health and much given to physicking himself, who combined the function of Home and Foreign Secretaries with those of head of MI5 and the Special Branch. It is on his performance in the latter capacities that Walsingham's notoriety depends.[4]

The secret service inherited by Robert Cecil from Walsingham was on a modest scale, its resources being actually reduced to £1,200 after the crisis of 1588 but its task in watching the Catholic community was not immense. There were only 5,560 convicted of recusancy in 1605 and only 112 of these were landowners subject to the two-thirds fine. The known activists, the noblemen and gentlemen who had been associated with Essex in his rebellion, were a mere handful.

When Walsingham died in 1590, the new Secretary of State was Robert Cecil (1563?–1612), Lord Burghley's younger son. Born to a political career, and given an early training in diplomacy, he was a small man and said to be a hunchback. He may not have been as great a man as his father but he was extremely able, very secret and (on occasion) quite ruthless. Under James I who was very idle, he had to bear the whole burden of administration. He was feared by his contemporaries but he had his close friends, the Earl of Suffolk being one and George Carew another. One of his great admirers was the Earl of Dorset, Lord Treasurer, in whose will Cecil, now Earl of Salisbury, is mentioned in these words:

When I behold the heavy weight of so many grave and great affairs which the special duty of his place as principal secretary doth daily and necessarily cast upon him, and do note withal what infinite cares, crosses, labours and travails both of body and mind he doth thereby continually sustain and undergo; and, lastly, do see with how great dexterity, sincerity and judgement he doth accomplish and perform the painful service of that place, these divine virtues of his so incessantly exercised and employed for the good of the public . . . have made me long since so greatly to love, honour and esteem him . . . that I do daily and heartily pray unto Almighty God to continue all strength and ability both of mind and body in him that he sink not under the weight of so heavy a burden . . . (He is of) so sweet a nature, so full of mildness, courtesy, honest mirth, bounty, kindness, gratitude and good discourse, so easily reconciled to his foe and enemies, so true unto his friends . . .[5]

That was one side of Salisbury, as seen by his friends. He had another side. We would do well to remember, however, that while our present concern is with a single conspiracy, one to which we can devote our whole attention for the time we spend in reading about it, he was not so fortunate. He had fifty other matters to consider, many of them more important, and could give to the plot a mere fraction of his time. He did the work of a modern Prime Minister and Foreign Secretary but he was also much concerned with finance, James being appallingly extravagant and Parliament in no mood to be generous. As successor, however, to Sir Francis Walsingham that 'most subtle searcher of secrets', Cecil was not without expert help. His right-hand man, so far as espionage was concerned, was Sir William Wade (or Waad), born in 1564. Son of Armagal Wade, 'the English Columbus' who sailed to Newfoundland in the time of Henry VIII, William was in the Cecils' service from the age of twenty. After much diplomatic experience he became ambassador to Portugal in 1580. In 1583 he became Clerk to the Privy Council and was foremost in the investigation of the different plots against Elizabeth and James I. While still Clerk to the Privy Council he became Lieutenant of the Tower of London in 1605. He was known to be expert in the field of interrogation for which his work at the

9

Tower was to give him scope. Philip Caraman says of him that 'He was feared only less than Popham for his venom against Catholics.' Next in importance to Wade was Phelippes, secretary to Salisbury himself, whose speciality was in decoding messages written in cipher. He had played an important part in the Babington Plot, as we shall see, and especially in the interception and deciphering of Mary Stuart's correspondence. He is thought to have been the brain behind the government spy system. A very different character was Richard Topcliffe (1532–1604), the jailer of the Gatehouse Prison, known for his cruelty to Robert Southwell and other Catholic prisoners. He was dead before the time of the Gunpowder Plot but he had played a great part in setting up a system which was to outlive him. It was a system in which the use of torture played an important part. The equipment normally used was the rack, and the Rackmaster at the Tower of London was responsible for applying pressure in this form. In studying the treason trials of the period we have always to remember that much of the evidence had been extracted by torture from both witnesses and the accused. And even when no torture was used, all were aware of the possibility and were eager to give the sort of evidence which would be acceptable. The rack was a device by which the victim was pulled lengthwise to the point at which his arms and legs would be dislocated. Its convenience lay in the fact that the skilled operator could adjust the agony with some precision, beginning with a relatively mild treatment and proceeding, if necessary, to greater severity. It needed an exceptionally resolute man to withstand much of it, and it was often enough just to allow the prisoner to see the rack. There were some limitations on its use, however. It was seldom applied to nobles or gentlemen of any consequence. It was applied, however, to Catholics, whether laymen or priests, and was thought especially useful in gaining evidence to use against Jesuits.

During the Earl of Salisbury's time the centre of power, under the queen, lay in the Privy Council. Its members included such personalities as the Lord Treasurer, Lord Dorset; the Lord Chancellor, Sir Thomas Egerton; the Lord Admiral, Lord Howard of Effingham, Earl of Nottingham after 1597; the Lord Chamberlain, the Earl of Suffolk; the Archbishop of Canterbury, John Whitgift, succeeded by Richard Bancroft in 1604; and the Captain of the Guard, Sir Walter Raleigh. Below Council level were the other officers of the household and a vague outer fringe of courtiers, men who attended court without holding any actual office. And just as the monarch was surrounded by noblemen in attendance, each of these noblemen was surrounded in turn by his gentlemen, the officers of his household. It is the word 'gentleman' we have now to understand. We may have been brought up to believe that it defines a man with certain moral qualities. In sixteenth- and seventeenth-century England it served rather to indicate a man's position in society. On a high level were the noblemen, and inferior to them were the knights. Below them came those entitled to be called esquire. A man so called was one eligible for knighthood who had not, so far, received the accolade. He was eligible because his income, derived from the land he owned, came to something like £200 or £300 a year. That figure is significant in revealing the value of money at that time. In 1597 William Shakespeare paid £60 for New Place, a large house in the centre of Stratford-on-Avon. To have £200 a year, therefore, was to be a man of some consequence. Many esquires had a great deal more than that, as we know, but some £200 per annum was their minimum level, below which they could not support the dignity which went with their title.

Below the esquires came the gentlemen. In a letter or on a tombstone they had not 'Esquire' but 'Gentleman' or 'Gent' after their name. Experts in protocol actually subdivided 'gentlemen' into nine different categories, the highest being gentlemen of ancestry, the second being gentlemen of blood and so on down to categories which were only marginally superior to yeomen. With a vague memory of Victorian squires, we feel that an Elizabethan gentleman should have had a manor house, a village under his influence and a suitably deferential group of tenants. All this he often had but a single manor would seldom go far to meet his needs. Noblemen had vast and scattered estates, with whole villages they had never seen except as names on a rent-roll. There were wealthy squires whose income was comparable. But the man with but the single manor was faced with the problem of making a living. He was often a younger son, brother to a man of real wealth, bearing a good name and a coat of arms. The English system of primogeniture by which the elder brother took all, might leave the next son with a small property left him by his aunt and the youngest son with nothing at all. A gentleman was sometimes even an elder son whose father threatened to outlive him, a man of expectations but heavily in debt. These were young men who had been brought up in comfortable surroundings, men who had perhaps been to the university or the inns of court, men who felt entitled to mingle on equal terms with their more fortunate relatives and schoolfellows. Below these in general esteem were men whose position was more marginal, sons of well-educated and respectable parents who had gained position but not an estate. The 'professional' class at this period was quite small, comprising only the higher ranks of the clergy – canons, archdeacons and bishops – the holders of a doctorate, a few successful physicians and a few established lawyers. All these were gentlemen of a sort but in professions which did not particularly attract the younger son. William Shakespeare was a gentleman, being a royal servant and also, on a small scale, a landowner. There was no regular career in the army or navy and the parish clergy were not yet regarded as gentlemen at all.

Gentlemen with pretensions but little regular income, young men with a horse and a sword and little else, might hope some day to marry an heiress. In the meanwhile, they hung about court, lodged in obscure backstreets off the Strand, and hoped that their more prosperous relatives would ask them to dine. It was a period when people in society were all related, more or less, to everyone else. The world of those to be regarded as gentlefolk was relatively small and early death allowed the survivors to marry two or three times, thus widening their circle of relatives. Youngsters without money would attach themselves, in the first instance, to the household of some prosperous nobleman or knight. They were described, first of all, as 'page' or even 'footman' and did little more than add to their patron's consequence. As they became more useful, however, some of them obtained more recognized positions as steward, secretary or master of the horse. A nobleman of real importance would thus have a group of gentlemen at his heels, the older among them having work to do, sometimes of great importance, and the younger being at least well-dressed and armed. They would begin to gain wider experience if their master became an ambassador or went to war. Some in this way gained a military reputation or a knowledge of foreign languages. Some might end in the employ of the queen herself.

For a fortunate few of these gallants some official provision had been made. In addition to the Yeomen of the Guard, the monarch had the Gentlemen Pensioners:

There are in all fifty gentlemen, besides the Captain, the Lieutenant, the Clerk of the Cheque and Gentleman Harbinger, including some of the best and ancientest families in England and some of the sons of earls and barons, knights and esquires, all thereunto specially recommended by their fitness in office, without any strain or taint of dishonour or disparagement. Both the late Queen and her predecessors have had great use of the service, in the guard and defence of their royal persons, as also in other employment, as well civil as military, at home and abroad; insomuch that it has served them always as a nursery for the breeding up of Deputies of Ireland, Ambassadors into foreign parts, Councillors of State, Captains of the Guard, Governors of places and Commanders in the wars, both by land and by sea . . .[6]

These fortunate men were paid a salary and might be supposed to have the chance of a possibly distinguished career. It will be noticed that the emphasis, in selecting them, was on good family and good character. There were other and wilder young men whose character was not without stain or taint of dishonour. They were apt to intrigue and quarrel, gamble and drink. When their claims for employment were pointedly ignored their best plan was to serve in a campaign or two in the Low Countries. Military experience could be gained on either side in any war and the youngster might return with a fluency in Spanish and some reputation for gallantry in the field. He might eventually be brought to notice in a favourable sense. As against that, he was as likely to end in prison or be killed in a duel. There were gallants enough round the fringes of the court and some wastage among them would hardly be noticed.

2

The Plot Thickens

UNDER the administration of the Cecils, whether the father or the son, there was a treasonable plot every five or ten years. As between one plot and the next there was a certain similarity. There was, to begin with, a nucleus conspiracy, usually involving some contact with France or Spain. The existence of the plot became known to Walsingham, partly through his agents and partly because one conspirator betrayed the others. There followed a very public crisis, with the queen and her ministers in palpable danger but saved by the timely intervention of providence. The conspirators were then brought to public trial and led from that to an even more public execution, with penitent speeches from the scaffold. Mere accomplices might be sent to the pillory. It then became apparent that some eminent but superfluous public figure had been implicated in the plot and must be tried in his turn. After this sensational climax to Act III there followed an Epilogue in which the government told the story (but not all of it) and pointed the moral at possibly tedious length. The darkest treacheries had been brought to light. The most sinister treason had been frustrated. Justice had been done and God had once more saved the queen.

A relatively early sensation of this kind was the Ridolphi Plot of 1570. Roberto di Ridolphi was a Florentine banker who had settled in London and did business there as a financier. After the northern rebellion of 1569 he was arrested as a suspected participant but was released for lack of evidence. There was a new plot, however, in 1570 with the object of preparing the way for a Spanish invasion.

Ridolphi's agent, Charles Baillie, was arrested at Dover when he himself was at Brussels, from which city he finally returned to Florence. It is impossible here to go into all the complexities of the story but one feature of special interest is the part played by Henry Brooke, Lord Cobham, whose sister married Sir Robert Cecil. Apparently involved in the conspiracy, he was arrested and sent to the Tower but was released again shortly and restored to high office. It would seem more than probable that he and his disreputable brother were both used as agents by Sir William Cecil. It finally became apparent that the Duke of Norfolk also had been a party to the conspiracy and that his object was to marry the Queen of Scots.

By the time the Queen of Scots fled to England in the summer of 1568, the Duke of Norfolk was already by repute the richest man in England, as well as the highest peer, and a widower. There seemed to be no insurmountable obstacle in the path of the fourth, last, and most promising of the Duke's matrimonial ventures. It was not absurd or far-fetched and certainly involved in itself no disloyalty ... Long before the autumn of 1569, however, Sir William Cecil and his friends had been completely alienated by Norfolk's opposition to their Spanish policy in the Privy Council. The Duke's influence had threatened at more than one point to bring about Cecil's political destruction, or at least eclipse. Cecil, not less ambitious than Norfolk, and a good deal more capable, could not afford to ignore the challenge. Skilfully, he span a web about the feet of Norfolk as he went blandly on his way – or so the surviving evidence strongly suggests. Norfolk, himself, preoccupied with his latest dream, co-operated with his rival in almost every move ... In truth, the Duke never swerved in his loyalty to Elizabeth, but considering all the circumstances, there is nothing surprising in the fact that in the early days of October, 1569, the Duke was conducted to the Tower of London as a prisoner of State.[1]

The Duke, then the only man of that rank in England, was indicted for planning to marry the Queen of Scots and for seeking to compass the death of Queen Elizabeth by waging war against her in alliance with divers aliens and foreigners. His conviction of treason was more or less automatic, as was his sentence of death. Whether Elizabeth would sign the death warrant was another matter, but there was revealed (at exactly the right moment) yet another plot. The slightly improbable conspirators were Kenelm Berney and

Edmund Mather, 'a brace of authentic pantomime villains', both of them gentlemen about court. They were closely watched from the outset by a government spy called Herle. A few days before the Duke's trial, 16 January 1572, the Principal Secretary, Lord Burghley, received an anonymous letter from an apparently penitent assassin.

My Lord, of late I have upon discontent entered into conspiracy with some others to slay your Lordship ... And being touched with some remorse of so bloody a deed ... I warn your Lordship of the evil ... and would further declare the whole meaning ... For the thanks I deserve I shall, I doubt not, but receive them hereafter at your hands, at more convenient time when the storms are past ...[2]

The conspirators were executed and so was the Duke, and Walsingham wrote that 'I perceive through God's good Providence your Lordship hath escaped the danger of a most devilish Italian practice.' The official angle on the affair was summarized by Sir Francis Walsingham in a pamphlet entitled *A Discourse touching the pretended Match between the Duke of Norfolk and the Queen of Scots.* A sequel to this drama was the elimination of the Howard family from the struggle for power. Thomas Howard, the 4th Duke, had been a rival to Lord Burghley. More than that, he had represented the old nobility, members of which looked down upon the Cecils as upstarts. The Howards were numerous and some of them were to be active in politics, but they were now subordinate to the Cecils. They had still a part to play but they had learnt their lesson. A further sequel was that other members of the old nobility had learnt something by Norfolk's example. If he had failed, what chance had they? If he had been executed, who might be spared? The loyalty of the Howards would no longer be in question.

We come now to the Babington Plot of 1587. Anthony Babington (aged about twenty-five) had been page to Lord Shrewsbury and so brought into contact with Mary, Queen of Scots during her captivity at Sheffield. He afterwards came to London and made friends there with other Catholics, even forming a society in 1580 for the protection of Jesuits in England. He was a squire of some wealth, with valuable land and property, no mere gentleman about town. He afterwards travelled on the continent where he met a Catholic priest called Ballard. Between them, they devised a harebrained plan for the murder of Elizabeth and for her replacement by Mary, Queen of Scots. After travelling in England in November 1585, Ballard reported that the English Catholics were ready to rise in revolt. He had spoken with Lord Henry Howard, with Lord Arundel (in the Tower), with the Earl of Northumberland, Lord Strange, Lord Stourton, Lord Darcy, Lord Compton and Lord Windsor. Other adherents he named included Lord Vaux, Sir Thomas Tresham and Sir William Catesby. Whether these were more than generally sympathetic may be doubted but Ballard was confident and Babington recruited five young gentlemen who had access to the court and agreed to kill the queen, Lord Burghley, Sir Francis Walsingham, Lord Hunsdon and Sir F. Knollys. One of the young gallants, Charles Tilney, was a Gentleman Pensioner; another, Edmund Abingdon, was son of the Under-Treasurer. Babington was not himself a member of this group, having assigned himself the task of rescuing Mary, Queen of Scots. Sequel to the murder would be the landing of a Spanish army but this part of the plot was rather vague. Ballard, in Paris, explained the whole scheme to Thomas Morgan, Mary's representative there, and also to Gilbert Gifford, a known Catholic of a good Staffordshire family. Unfortunately for the success of the scheme, Gifford was a member of the English secret service. With all agreed in outline, Morgan now decided to tell Mary, Queen of Scots, what was happening. His letter contained a passing reference to the fate which awaited Elizabeth; not explicit, perhaps, but sufficiently clear. 'There be many means in hand,' he wrote, 'to remove the beast that troubles all the world.' Mary had been moved, meanwhile, from Sheffield to Tutbury, her jailer being Sir Amyas Paulet, a far stricter man than Shrewsbury had been. From there she was moved to Chartley Manor, the Earl of Essex's house in south Derbyshire. She was allowed no uncensored correspondence with the outer world but Gifford set up for her a secret system of communication, letters coming and going in casks from the local brewery at Burton. These were copied and deciphered by

Walsingham's secretary before being sent on as directed. Receiving Morgan's letter and another, still more imprudent, from Babington, Mary replied at length, conveying her frank approval of the plot and discussing in some detail the plan for her own release. Walsingham now knew of the plot in outline and lacked only a complete list of names:

Walsingham was still in great uncertainty. Ballard, supposing Gifford to know more than he did, talked to him with considerable unreserve. Gifford had gathered that his and Babington's accomplices were persons near about the Queen. They were followed at night if they went abroad, and their houses watched to discover by whom they were visited . . .

Walsingham was in no haste. Gifford told him that he had been directed by Ballard to go to Spain, to learn when a fleet might be looked for on the coast, and that till his return no active attempt would be made. He wanted more precise information. He now knew that there were six persons who were to act against the Queen, and that Babington was not one of them, for Babington was to rescue the Queen of Scots. He had discovered that twelve or fourteen young gentlemen were in the habit of supping together, or meeting at each other's houses, and that among these the six would be found . . .

Never were men engaged in so desperate a service more infatuated idiots, and never had Mary Stuart's genius failed her more egregiously than in trusting them. Unsuspicious of the eyes that were upon them, and full of careless confidence . . . [the conspirators continued to sup together] . . . On the 3rd–13th August they had a sudden alarm. A servant of Ballard's who knew more than was good for them, was discovered to have been in the pay of the Government. The base material of which Babington was made instantly revealed itself. Caitiff at heart in the midst of his bravado, he wrote the same day to Pooley, one of Walsingham's staff, bidding him tell Walsingham that there was a conspiracy in hand, and that he was prepared to reveal it.[3]

The seditious group disintegrated and the conspirators fled, Babington and four others being captured while hiding in the thickets of St John's Wood. They were caught, tried and executed. Babington's estate went to Sir Walter Raleigh who thus became (for the first time) a landowner. What was more important, Burghley now had the evidence on which Mary, Queen of Scots, could be brought to trial. Just as the Ridolphi Plot was fatal to the Duke of

Norfolk, so was the Babington Plot fatal to Mary Stuart. Following her trial, she was beheaded at Fotheringay Castle on 8 February 1587.

We come, last of all, to the Earl of Essex's rebellion in 1601. As she neared the end of her reign, Queen Elizabeth was much concerned, as we are today, with the situation in Ulster. To deal with the rebel Tyrone, Elizabeth's intention was to send over Sir William Knollys or Sir Charles Blount. Her favourite, the Earl of Essex, objected to either appointment and found himself given the command. As the queen was angry with him at the time, it was a question in his mind whether he was expected to win or whether the campaign was meant to be his last. His absence in the field would give his enemies the chance to intrigue against him, and Ireland, as he knew, had been the grave of many other military reputations. He went to Dublin in April 1599, and had at his command an army of 1,300 cavalry and 16,000 infantry. Instead of moving against Tyrone, however, as he had been ordered to do, he tried to conquer Munster first. By the time he turned to Ulster, his forces had dwindled through sickness and desertion. Instead of fighting, therefore, he negotiated with Tyrone and finally signed a treaty of peace. To make matters still worse, he returned, unbidden, to London, anxious to explain away his failure to the queen. She was furious with him, rejected his explanation and deprived him of his command. In June 1600, he was tried before a special commission which found him guilty of various offences but, above all, for disobedience of orders. He was deprived of his public offices and lost, to his enemy Sir Walter Raleigh, the monopoly of sweet wines which had been his main source of income. Essex was furious in turn and began to talk sedition. Of the queen he is said to have remarked that her mind was as crooked as her body.

He threw open his house to discontented persons of all kinds, adventurers, soldiers out of employ, puritan preachers. In February 1601 plans for the coup d'état were concocted at Drury House, the residence of his principal supporter, the Earl of Southampton. It was believed that he could calculate on a following of 120, composed of two earls, Southampton and Rutland, several barons, and a large number of gentlemen . . .[4]

On 7 February 1601, the Earl was summoned to appear before the Council. He refused to come, pleading sickness. Next day, Sunday, he collected his adherents at Essex House and told them that Lord Cobham and Sir Walter Raleigh were plotting to take his life. It is important to realize at this point that Essex was known to be an advocate of tolerance, extending it to both Catholics and Puritans. His followers therefore included a fair proportion of Catholics, who looked to him for a relaxation of the laws which oppressed them. His chief adherent, the 3rd Earl of Southampton, Shakespeare's patron, was not himself an avowed Catholic but was the son of the 2nd Earl, who had been sent to the Tower for connivance in the Catholic Plot of 1569 to marry the Duke of Norfolk to Mary, Queen of Scots. The Earl of Rutland was no Catholic but was at this time little more than a boy, aged twenty-three. Sir Christopher Blount had been Essex's Marshal (or Chief of Staff) in Ireland. William Parker, heir to Lord Morley, was a young man of good family, aged twenty-six. Among the gallants of lesser importance were Robert Catesby, Francis Tresham, John Grant and John Wright. Catesby was the son of Sir William Catesby, one of the Catholic recusants listed as a potential supporter of Mary, Queen of Scots. Francis Tresham, who may have been at Oxford with Catesby, was the son of Sir Thomas Tresham, who had been imprisoned for seven years for harbouring the Jesuit Campion. John Grant was another Catholic and John Wright, of the same Church and a close friend of Catesby, was supposed to be among the best swordsmen of the day. The malcontents would seem to have numbered about three hundred in all. When Essex led this riotous mob towards the City the number fell to about two hundred. There was no response in London to his wild appeals for support and he turned back towards the Strand. His way was blocked by troops under the command of Sir John Leveson and he returned by river to find Essex House already besieged. There would seem to have been some desultory fighting in which John Wright was said to have been conspicuous, and then the end came and Essex surrendered. He was tried for treason and inevitably condemned to death. Five of his followers, Blount included, were also beheaded or hanged.

Southampton and Rutland were pardoned and others were lucky indeed to escape the gallows. Catesby escaped with a fine of £3,000 and sold his Chastleton estate in order to pay it. Francis Tresham would have been hanged but for the intercession of Lady Catherine Howard, daughter of Lord Thomas Howard who later became the Earl of Suffolk. His life was spared but his father, Sir Thomas, had to pay for him a fine of at least £2,000. Others escaped more lightly, either because they were young, or because they had no money. Elizabeth was lenient, on the whole, with the foolish men who had followed a foolish leader.

It cannot be said that the Essex Rebellion is a good example, in itself, of the Elizabethan conspiracy. Burghley and Walsingham were both dead by this time and the task of dealing with Essex fell essentially to Burghley's son, Sir Robert Cecil, Secretary of State. He had the same technique as Walsingham, whose secret service he had inherited, but the Essex affair presented no challenge to his detectives. All was known from the outset, Essex shouting from the housetops what a wiser man would have whispered in a dark corner. Care was taken not to interfere too soon but the problem after that was relatively simple. There were some problems at the trial but these were dealt with in masterly fashion by Sir Robert's cousin, Francis Bacon. Essex's treason admitted of little defence and the affair is mainly of interest as another example of the mighty laid low. Once more an example had been made and a warning given to all other potential traitors. Treason would not be forgiven, not even in one who had been the queen's closest friend. Even her favourite was still her subject and was expected as such to obey her orders. She was an old woman now and with but a short time to live, but she remained in power until she died, her throne more or less secure from the time of Mary's death. Her named successor, Mary's son, was a Protestant and the negotiations were going on, without her knowledge, which would put James on the throne without any hint of dispute or doubt. Still resolute in some ways, still vacillating in others, magnificent but exasperating to the end, she finally died on 24 March 1603.

From a study of these three examples we can perceive a certain pattern in the conspiracies of this period. What is apparent, first of all, is that each plot was put to good use by those in power. The experienced public speaker does not resent the interruption shouted by someone at the back of the hall. He rather welcomes it as an opportunity to show his quickness in riposte. There is a quick and deadly retort, a roar of homeric laughter, and the incident is over. 'As I was saying—' the orator continues, but with enhanced prestige and to a more responsive audience. In much the same way Lord Burghley or his son would welcome a conspiracy, watching it with paternal approval, giving it a little discreet help, steering it in the right direction and shattering it with utmost publicity and at exactly the right moment. Some authors have ventured to suggest that some conspiracies were wholly fictitious. Of this there is no proof and our conclusion must be that the Cecils, father and son, were never as crude as that. Nor was it likely that many years would pass without some halfwit attempting some treasonable stupidity. Once identi-fied, however, the plot had to serve some wider and deeper purpose. Its more immediate effects would involve the execution of those who were to have committed the crime, but these were often people of no position or ability, whose life or death was a triviality. Its less im-mediate effects were to discredit, weaken or ruin someone of impor-tance; a person who was supposed to have instigated the conspiracy or for whose benefit the treason had been planned. In this context we would do well to take note of a letter written by Sir Walter Raleigh to Sir Robert Cecil, undated but plainly dating from the time (February–August 1600) when Essex's fate was still in doubt:

... I am not wise enough to give you advice; but if you take it for a good counsel to relent towards this tyrant (Essex) you will repent it when it shall be too late. His malice is fixed and will not evaporate by any of your mild courses. For he will ascribe the alteration to her Majesty's pusillanimity and not to your good nature; knowing that you work but upon her honour, and not out of any love towards him. The less you make him, the less he shall be able to harm you and yours. And if her Majesty's favour fail him, he will again decline to be a common person. For after revenges, fear them not. For if your own father that was esteemed to be the contriver of Norfolk's ruin, yet his son followeth your father's son, and loveth him.[5]

Cecil had no need of this letter from Essex's known enemy. Essex was in any case to go the way Norfolk had gone. It is of interest, however, in illustrating the fact that no quarter was given in the struggle for power. It is also interesting that Cecil, in so far as he took advice, applied it to Raleigh himself.

But more distant results are still more worthy of study. First of all, the plot and its sequel conveyed a message to a public which was difficult to reach in any other way. Ours is an age of radio and television, newspapers and film, an age which makes us peculiarly vulnerable to announcement or exhortation. We are all too familiar with the face and voice of each leading politician and it is hard to avoid hearing his views for what they are worth. Elizabethan statesmen had more obvious ability but were far less fortunate in their means of communication. They could address one or other House of Parliament and hope that rumour would carry their message to a wider audience. Through the Church a government was able to convey the sort of simple announcement that could be made from the pulpit; a thanksgiving for victory, say, or the celebration of some special event. An official document might be printed for circulation but its message would never reach the many people who were illiterate. Of all the means of publicity available the best was unquestionably the public trial, and of all such trials the best was one in which the charge was that of treason. The case for the Crown was not merely addressed to the Judge and Jury; it was directed to the people or indeed to the world. The words of the Attorney-General would spread through the city by word of mouth. The confession of the person accused might be repeated in a hundred sermons in as many churches. The words of condemnation would travel as fast and so would the words of penitence uttered at the foot of the gallows. To convey a simple message like 'Down with the Jesuits' or 'God has saved the Queen' there was nothing as dramatic as a public execution. The event was staged so as to make the message clear, and a conspiracy had this further merit: that the executions need not all take place at the same spot. Were the victim of sufficiently high rank, moreover, the message would even go overseas, the news item too important to overlook. To let it be known that the Queen of

23

Scots was not being considered as a possible successor to Queen Elizabeth might not, in itself, cause great excitement. To announce that 'The Queen of Scots has been beheaded' would at least gain attention; and this was one argument for using the axe rather than a mere proclamation. People would have to admit that the point had been made.

The man convicted of treason was not merely sentenced to death but to a horrible death, revolting in its cruelty. He was to be hanged, drawn and quartered; disembowelled, indeed, while supposedly alive. We may see in this the ultimate expression of public vengeance on a traitor; nor can we doubt that revenge played a great part in it. But it was not mere cruelty for the sake of cruelty. The infliction of that sentence was also a means of securing wider publicity. The condemned man was drawn through the streets on a hurdle, a painful degradation which would be seen by a maximum number of people – by far more than could see the execution itself. The gallows might be high but higher still, and seen by those more distant, was the smoke which ascended from the fire into which the wretched man's parts had been thrown. The body was finally hacked into quarters – a part of the sentence which took place after death – no doubt with some religious significance but also in order that the four parts might be exhibited in as many different places. The effect of the whole grisly exhibition was to show what would happen to one who conspired against the sovereign. The public was invited to join in detestation of the man who had been ready to betray his country. If all went well he would emphasize the lesson by admitting his guilt on the scaffold and acknowledging the justice of his sentence. Publicity was the essence of the whole affair and it was a publicity which could have been achieved in no other way. The trial and execution would be something in which people would share; it was also, better still, a lesson they would remember.

The trial also served another purpose. The conspiracy, it would appear, had been revealed by some almost miraculous chance. A conspirator at the last moment had felt remorse and was moved to betray his friends. A strange letter had been received, no one at first able to guess its exact meaning. God was on the government's side and had intervened to prevent so horrible a crime. For the common folk, for the broadsheet, for the preacher, this was the divine process by which all had been dramatically revealed. For the courtiers and for the foreign ambassadors, for the merchants and gentry, there was a different message. They might not so readily believe in God's contribution to the detective work. They were more likely to conclude that Lord Burghley was a man of incomparable ability (as indeed he was) and that Walsingham's spies were everywhere. The story about divine protection was all very well and just the thing to strengthen the common people's confidence in the regime, but the real truth was that Burghley and Walsingham had known all about the plot from its inception. The conspirators had been watched and followed, their mail had been intercepted, their conversations had been privily overheard. They wrote to each other in code but each message had been deciphered by an expert. They had trusted their servants but these had been won over by threats and bribes. When questioned, they had lied, contradicting themselves and each other. When shown the rack, they had broken down and confessed all. What a skilful operation it had been! Ministers had received early warning but had been in no hurry to make arrests. They had waited patiently until all the traitors had revealed themselves, until the right moment had come. Then they had acted with resolution and speed, pouncing at the exact moment when the intending assassin was loading his weapon or sharpening his dagger. In an instant they had trapped all the conspirators and all the evidence. Burghley was no fool, as all had to admit, and Walsingham was not asleep at his desk. Honest men could rest assured that the regime was secure, that the sentinels were alert, that our enemies would always be outwitted. Fully to understand that sense of assurance we need to contrast the sixteenth with the twentieth century. We are faced with the same sort of situation, but the well-meaning people who appear on television are the very picture of twittering ineptitude. We have no reason to be confident of their final victory and would be startled, indeed, to hear of their transient success. The Elizabethans were more fortunate. They had the pleasant feeling that their rulers were pretty certain to outmanoeuvre their opponents; a feeling we last felt during World War Two. The Elizabethan achievement in literature and music, in architecture and on the stage had as its background a certain confidence in their government. All might be at risk and all too much might depend upon a single life, but they were not going to face disaster as a result of sheer incompetence.

So the revealed conspiracy was a demonstration of skill. It conveyed a warning to traitors at home and to enemies abroad. But no attempt was made to exterminate the possible rebels in advance. Still less was it the policy to execute all possible accomplices at the time. Certain of those guilty were executed with a calculated show of cold-blooded ferocity. Some of those who might have been involved but against whom the evidence was weak, men who were regarded as generally dangerous, were as pitilessly brought to the gallows or the block. But there was no senseless massacre, no thirst for blood as such. A man might die but his estate might still go to his widow and children. A young man who clearly deserved death might be let off with a fine. Some who might have been arrested were apparently ignored. Mercy, like severity, was a matter of calculation and policy. Enemies spared today might be useful allies tomorrow. This was more obviously true of the younger men, gallants who were dissatisfied, bored and ready for mischief. Why be too hard on them? An army in which every insubordinate subaltern is cashiered would soon cease to exist. But there were other dissidents, older men who were neither high-spirited nor drunk, men of a more serious character whose loyalty was in doubt. Should they not be eliminated before they could join in some other plot? The answer was 'No'. The great thing was that they had been identified. When it became apparent that a new conspiracy was being hatched, these were the men to suspect. In the search for the really dangerous men, these malcontents would provide a point of departure. They would not be at the very centre of the movement but their comings and goings could be noted. Were they seeing much of some new friends? Were they in or out of town for no particular reason? Did they seem to be bursting with some new sense of importance? If they were to be the dupes of other and more sinister characters, it would be they (not their mentors) who would talk in their cups. To have such people around might be very useful indeed. It would be even more useful, perhaps, to have the names of some more important people who had done something treasonable in the past but who had been forgiven. For these would be vulnerable, after all, to pressure. On the other hand, their past record might gain for them the confidence of those who might be ignorant of their more recent change of heart. That they would act, to some extent, as double agents could be assumed – Walsingham and his staff knew all about that – but the first clue to a new conspiracy might come from just such a nobleman, knight or esquire. With the sort of information Walsingham possessed it would have been possible to suppress each plot at the outset. But this was never the policy. To make the best use of a conspiracy, the accepted plan was to watch and wait. As Walsingham observed: 'Knowledge is never too dearly bought.'

3

The Scottish King

WHEN the bell of St Giles's Church, Edinburgh, rang out for two o'clock on the morning of 10 February 1567, there was a deafening explosion in the outskirts of the city. By first light it became known generally that the old house at Kirk O'Fields (on the site of what is now the old quadrangle of the University of Edinburgh) had been completely destroyed. Its tenant at that moment was Henry Stuart, Lord Darnley and Duke of Albany, not yet recognized as King Henry of Scotland. It then transpired that Darnley had not been blown up. He and his page had been strangled and their bodies were found in the garden. The queen had planned to be there that night but changed her mind at the last moment. Darnley had been at Glasgow, where he was safe among his Lennox clansmen, but Mary had him brought to Edinburgh so that he could publicly recognize his son, the future King James VI of Scotland. He was ill at the time, officially with smallpox but probably in fact with syphilis. In bringing him to Edinburgh, she lodged him in an insecure place, close to the home of his feudal foes, the Hamiltons. He had been, like Mary was to be, a prisoner in England but Elizabeth allowed him to go to Scotland in 1565, in which year he married the queen but was not given the status of king. His importance, it has been said, was almost wholly genealogical, he having a strong claim to the Scottish throne in his own right. When he came north by Mary's invitation he was aged nineteen, without any money and without a single friend. The marriage was a reality for about six months but was then destroyed by political

28

stresses, by Darnley's infidelity and by his fondness for the bottle.

It seems unlikely, in retrospect, that the Italian David Riccio was or had ever been Mary's lover but he had gained great political influence and had practically superseded Maitland of Lethington as Secretary of State. Worse still, he excluded Darnley from political power. A band of the Scottish nobles, with Darnley among them, seized him in Mary's presence and then killed him in the antechamber. Darnley made haste to betray his allies but his own guilt was obvious. As from that time his life was finished and it was only a question of when and how. To the question 'When?' we know the answer. To the question 'How?' we have too many possible answers and none of them entirely convincing. According to one theory there were three simultaneous plots on the night of 9–10 February. Some of Darnley's men had put the gunpowder in the house with a view to murdering the queen. Bothwell blew it up when Darnley was there and the queen was not, his object being to marry her afterwards, as he did – the marriage lasting one month. But Darnley escaped before the explosion, only to be killed by Morton's Douglas followers, who had been approaching the place with a plan of their own. Or had the powder been put there by Sir James Balfour? Or was Darnley strangled by the servants of Archbishop Hamilton? We shall never know. The final result was to end Mary Stuart's reign in Scotland, leaving Darnley's son to be brought up as her successor under firmly Protestant influences.

An author who attempts to explain the Gunpowder Plot of 1605 has enough to do without attempting, in the same work, to explain anything else. He can be excused surely from elucidating the Casket Letters or from discovering what really happened at Kirk O'Fields. Nor is he under any obligation to describe Scottish politics during the minority and reign of King James vi. He must, however, record two incidents from that period. Bothwell made three attempts to gain control over James vi, the third attempt being in 1594 on which occasion he had joined forces with the Earl of Huntly.

In the autumn of 1594 the King moved up to Aberdeenshire, accompanied by leaders of the Kirk. Huntly had considerable forces but he was wisely not prepared to commit them against a basically friendly sovereign. Under pressure from Andrew Melville, the Presbyterian leader, the King ordered Strathbogie Castle to be blown up with gunpowder. Huntly was offered a full pardon if he would deliver up Bothwell to justice, but this he refused. [Bothwell fled to France and never returned to Scotland.]

The other incident was the alleged Gowrie Conspiracy. John Ruthven, Earl of Gowrie, was a political opponent to whom James owed large sums of money. His brother, Alexander Ruthven, was a gentleman of the bedchamber to the king. He is said to have been instrumental in persuading the king to visit the Earl of Gowrie at his house near Perth. An attempt was then made to kidnap the king or so it was said, as a result of which Alexander Ruthven was killed by Sir John Ramsay. Attempting to avenge his brother's death, the Earl of Gowrie was then killed by the king's followers. All this took place on Tuesday, 5 August 1600, which James thereafter looked upon as his lucky day. This story of a Scottish host's treachery (whether true or false) was in Shakespeare's mind, no doubt, when he wrote *Macbeth* in 1605.

James VI had a difficult role to play in Scotland, a country in which both nobles and Calvinist ministers had considerable power. His tastes were scholarly and his manners rather pedantic and he did well to survive among the forays and plots. He had something of an impediment of speech, no military reputation and no head for finance. He was excessively generous to his followers, liking to see them happy, and had a passion for hunting. He had decided views about religion and was ahead of his time in condemning the use of tobacco. He combined a firm belief in monarchy as established by God with a certain lack of dignity. When he concluded the Treaty of Berwick in 1586 he received a pension from Queen Elizabeth and was virtually recognized as heir to the throne of England, his mother's prior claim being set aside. He made formal protests when she was brought to trial but was far from inconsolable when she was executed. He married Anne of Denmark in 1589 and her children included Henry in 1594 and Charles in 1600. He was thus supremely eligible as Elizabeth's successor, being a firm Protestant, married, with male issue and years of experience as a ruler. There was only one other possible claimant, the Lady Arabella Stuart, but her claim was inferior to his. Sir Robert Cecil saw that James had to be king and did all he could to bring it about. He was in touch with James during Elizabeth's last years and the succession was not in question. There was, of course, tacit agreement that Sir Robert was to remain in office. He was careful at the same time to warn James against three men he regarded as dangerous: Lord Cobham, Sir Walter Raleigh and the 9th Earl of Northumberland. 'You must remember also that I gave you notice of the diabolical triplicity, that is Cobham, Raleigh and Northumberland, that met every day at Durham House . . . to watch what chicken they could hatch out of these cockatrice eggs that were daily and nightly sitten on.'

As for Northumberland, Lord Henry Howard wrote of him (for Cecil and no doubt in Cecil's words): 'The man is beloved of none, followed by none, trusted by no one nobleman or gentleman of quality within the land beside his faction.'

Of the three men, the most important was of course, Northumberland. Like Norfolk, he was a member of the old nobility and in a position to look down upon the Cecils. He held a great position as landowner in the north of England. Although not of their religion, he was regarded by many Catholics as their leader. This was a matter of family tradition for the 7th Earl was a Catholic favoured by Mary Tudor, who rebelled and was beheaded in 1572. The 8th Earl had intrigued on behalf of Mary, Queen of Scots and was sent to the Tower, where he apparently shot himself. The 9th Earl was less involved in politics, being an amateur scientist, but he was enough of a Catholic figurehead to plead with James (even before his accession) for a measure of tolerance in matters of religion. The man he sent on this mission was Thomas Percy, a distant relative whom he had appointed as steward and rent collector of his northern estates. This position was an important one and led to his ranking as an esquire. A native of Beverley in Yorkshire, Thomas was a man of consequence, having charge of Alnwick and Warkworth Castles. Although a Catholic he was presently made one of the Gentlemen Pensioners and so had at least a minor position at court. We know the result of Percy's mission from the Earl himself who stated afterwards that:

... When Percy came out of Scotland from the King (his Lordship having written to the King, where his advice was to give good hopes to the Catholics, that he might the more easily without impediment come to the crown), he said that the King's pleasure was, that his Lordship should give the Catholics hopes that they should be well dealt withal, or to that effect. James afterwards strenuously denied that he had ever authorized Percy to convey such a message to the Earl of Northumberland, or had ever given encouragement to the Roman Catholics to expect from him a relaxation of the penal laws against them; but the simple denial of James on a point of this kind is not entitled to much credit.[1]

His denial deserves the less credit in that he gave the same vague assurances to the French ambassador. When Elizabeth died, the Catholics were all on his side. He was proclaimed king in London and presently began a leisurely journey southward, staying with various nobles and finally with Cecil himself at Theobalds, on 3 May 1603. That was where (on 4 May) he held his first Council, retaining Elizabeth's Councillors but adding to their number Lord Henry Howard, the Duke of Lennox, the Earl of Mar, Sir George Home, Sir James Elphinston (Secretary of State for Scotland) and Lord Kinloss. 'The King hath declared, sitting in Council, that from henceforth he would not have the Council exceed the number of twenty-four persons.' A few days later Sir Walter Raleigh was replaced as Captain of the Guard by Sir Thomas Erskine, to the 'foul dudgeon' of Lord Cobham, who had wanted this appointment for himself. Two of Cecil's adversaries were thus dealt with at the very beginning of the new reign. There could be no doubt, therefore, that Cecil was still in power. As against that, the king was surrounded by Scotsmen and provision had to be made for them.

He has granted many of the highest offices to Scots. To the Earl of Mar he has handed the governnance both of his son, the prince of Wales, and of that province as well. He made Lord Home, a Scot, the governor of the town of Berwick ... Near his person everyone in his Chamber are Scots, wherever there is an English official he has placed another Scotsman. He has made a Scot named Thomas Erskine the Captain of his Guard . . . The Chancellor of the Duchy of Lancaster is a Scot. He has given bishopries to two Scotsmen . . .[2]

Fresh from the raids and stabbing affrays of Scotland, the rather nervous James wanted his bodyguard. He was, Sir John Oglander remarked, 'the most cowardly man that ever I knew'. His preference for his friends went beyond that, however, and became at once a scandal and a joke. In 1605 a play called *Eastward Ho* was put on at Blackfriars with a cast of children, the players making fun of Scotland and daring to mimic the king's accent. Hostility towards the Scots was more marked still in the north country and among Yorkshiremen, for example, to whom the Scots were the traditional enemy.

Elizabeth had been excommunicated by the Pope but this anathema was personal to her, as we have seen (p. 4), and did not extend automatically to her equally Protestant successor. To avert any such inconvenience James made friendly gestures towards the pope and showed his willingness to end the war with Spain. He was lenient, also, towards the Catholics in England, observing the promises that he afterwards denied having made. But here he encountered two difficulties. He had, to begin with, forgotten about Parliament, an institution unknown to him in Scotland. He could not repeal the laws directed against the Catholics except by Act of Parliament; and the House of Commons, as he soon came to realize, was utterly opposed to any such concession. And while he could and did relax the enforcement of the law, he soon came to realize that the fines paid by recusants, amounting to something under £5,000 a year, were a valuable source of income and that he needed the money if only to recompense the many poor men who had followed him south from Scotland. But James's relative tolerance was shown in other ways. Out hunting in Enfield Chase he was seen to 'be riding for the most part between the Earl of Northumberland and the Earl of Nottingham'. And when he visited the Tower, all the prisoners – 'of what quality soever, even Jesuits' – were set at liberty. The laws which oppressed the Catholics were still, however, in force. Catholics of great wealth – there were about a dozen of them – who failed to attend their parish church had to pay £20 per month. Catholic gentry of moderate wealth – some 162 of them when persecution was at its height – had to pay two-thirds of their yearly rental. Middle-class recusants had to pay a shilling a week. In deploring this severity we do well to remember that the collection of these fines was haphazard and negligent, many being able to avoid payment. We should also perhaps remember that the gentry today are fined much more heavily and much more consistently without having committed any offence of any kind. For the first years of his reign James let them off the fines to which they were liable, partly because of his promises (deny them as he might) and partly in recognition of the fact that they had not opposed his succession. Under pressure from the Council, James would eventually have hardened towards the Catholics in any case, but two conspiracies were now discovered which changed his attitude overnight. The revelation of these plots came at the right moment and involved the very people, strangely enough, against whom the king had been warned before he came to England.

In studying these plots, however briefly, we must note that, first of all, they closely follow the pattern established by Lord Burghley during the previous reign. A rather feeble-minded priest called William Watson was one of those who went to Scotland and accepted personal assurances from the king about better treatment for the Catholics. Finding on his return that Catholics were still to be penalized, he took counsel with another priest called William Clarke, as also with Mr George Brooke, Sir Griffin Markham and Lord Grey de Wilton. George Brooke was brother to Lord Cobham and Markham was related both to Babington and Lord Vaux of Harrowden. The plan was for a crowd of Catholics to rush into the royal presence and demand toleration from a presumably terrified king. Such was the split at the time between the seminary priests and the Jesuits that the outline of the plot was revealed to the government by the Archpriest Blackwell through the Bishop of London. All was also betrayed, no doubt, by Sir Griffin Markham with the result that George Brooke and the two priests were duly executed.

34

The trial then followed of Lords Cobham and Grey and Sir Griffin, all being likewise condemned to death. They were brought to the scaffold but reprieved at the last moment. A commentator remarked that 'It may rather seem to be a relation of a well-acted comedy . . .' although the comic side may not have been immediately appreciated by those on whom the joke was played. Cobham comes into theatrical history another way, however, for he it was who objected to Shakespeare's including Sir John Oldcastle in the cast of *Henry IV*, so compelling the dramatist to create Sir John Falstaff. This then was the Bye Plot, prelude to the Main Plot, which immediately followed. The effect of these plots was to ruin not only Cobham but also Sir Walter Raleigh.

. . . Ralegh was called in before the Council to say what he knew about Cobham's activities. After examination Ralegh wrote a disingenuous letter about Cobham's dealings with Arenberg, with regard to peace and pension from Spain, which clearly told less than he knew. That fatal flaw in his nature, the fact that he was a liar, gave a bad impression from the start, and from this time henceforth he was inextricably involved . . .

It has always been an unsolved mystery why an intelligent man like Ralegh should have put his head in the noose with a totally unstable psychotic type like Cobham . . .[3]

Mr Rowse goes on to suggest that Raleigh may well have joined the plot in order to betray it, and so indeed he might. Such a policy would, in theory, have led to Cobham's execution and Raleigh's regaining the king's favour. But that was no part of Cecil's plan. It was against Raleigh that the Chief Secretary was working and no other head would serve his purpose. In the upshot, Raleigh and Cobham were both condemned to death, both reprieved and both sent to the Tower. What is interesting about the affair, from our present point of view, is that the pattern of the conspiracy is already familiar. The plot is initiated by people of no great importance. Its ramifications extend so as to touch someone of note. The plot is betrayed to Cecil, probably by one of the conspirators. He bides his time, striking at the right moment, and all the plotters are arrested, tried, sentenced and publicly executed. The message is understood by the public at large, as also by foreign powers, and it indicated, in this instance, that the Elizabethan policy towards Catholics was still in force, despite anything the king may have said.

How the king's attitude changed towards the papists is illustrated by a news item of 1 November 1603:

Recusancy in the North

Of late there has been great increase of recusancy in the north since the penalty of the law has not been inflicted so absolutely as before, and many graces and favours have been shown to recusants. They begin to grow very insolent, and to show themselves more openly. Some go up and down to get a petition for toleration of religion. The Papists take it very kindly that the King has restored the Lords Arundel, Westmorland and Paget, all known favourers if not practisers of the Romish religion. Moreover, he has knighted sundry famous recusants; and others whose wives are recusants have been put into the Commission of the Peace.[4]

At this time, in 1603, James was intent on making peace with Spain and reaching an understanding with the pope. It was no time for prompt severity against the Catholics, however intolerant he meant to be. The immediate effect of his lenience, however, was to increase their apparent numbers. Those who had been lying low now revealed themselves. Those who had conformed occasionally now stayed away from church altogether. The policy, it was evident, would have to be reversed. Two events in 1604 now hastened the process. The first, which cannot be precisely dated, was the conversion of the queen to Catholicism. She had come to James from a Protestant background and there had been no reason to expect any such change of outlook. It may have been either the cause or result of the king and queen now living apart, with his homosexual tendencies becoming more widely known. To make matters worse, Sir John Lindsay went to Rome in November 1604 and had an audience with the pope at which he revealed without authority that the queen was already a Catholic and that James was ready to follow her example if satisfied on the question of papal supremacy. Rumours of this story reached Paris and it appeared that the pope was delighted, as indeed he must have been. James was furious, knowing that the story was going round the capitals of Europe. It came, moreover, at an unfortunate moment. James was attempting to suppress Puritanism with the inevitable result that he was suspected anyway of a leaning towards popery. The time had come to make his position clear and he did on 10 February 1605:

> Today being Sunday, the King made a long and vehement apology for himself in the Council Chamber against the Papists who flatter themselves with a vague hope of toleration, declaring that he never had any such intention . . . that the mitigation of their payments was in consideration that none of them had lifted up his hand against his coming in, and so he gave them a year of probation to conform themselves, which seeing it had wrought none effect he had fortified all the laws that were against them and made them stronger (saving for blood from which he had a natural aversion) and commanded that they should be put in execution to the uttermost.[5]

As a result of this changed policy some 5,560 persons were convicted of recusancy and 112 had to pay the full two-thirds of their annual rental. In the proclamation dated 22 February 1604, James had already 'commanded all Jesuits, Seminarists and other priests, to depart the realm before the 19th of March following and not to return, under the penalty of being left to the rigours of the law'. He now increased the pressure, with Cecil's full agreement, and showed confidence in his Secretary of State making him Viscount Cranborne and now (4 May) Earl of Salisbury.

It was clear to Salisbury that the Catholics would react to this pressure and indeed to their original disappointment in James. Their first instinct would be to seek help in Spain but here they were forestalled by James himself. Peace with Spain was the main feature of his foreign policy and the Spanish were still keener on making peace; so eager indeed that they would urge nothing which might upset the negotiations. Even in Elizabeth's time the Catholics, or some of them, the Jesuitical faction, had been hoping for a Spanish invasion. But this, as they discovered, was out of the question. Exhausted by the struggle in the Low Countries, the king of Spain's forces were unequal to any further effort against England. Whatever was to be done the English Catholics must do for themselves. Of this situation, Salisbury was perfectly aware. He could fairly assume that some sort of plot or rebellion was likely and a popish riot near Hereford on 23 May would have been enough to remind him that he must look out for symptoms of unrest. As for James he sent for the judges and told them to take strong measures against recusants, 'and as for the rebellious behaviour used in Herefordshire' he thought it needless 'to spare their blood who contemning his clemency have broken forth into so manifest a demonstration of their disloyalties towards his laws and his officers'. The time had come for drastic measures.

Salisbury was a man who moved secretly. We must not expect to find him announcing his plans at any sort of press conference. We know something of his resources, however, and something of his methods. He had inherited Walsingham's secret service and we hear of its continued activity. Catholic treasons were watched by a 'discoverer' called Davies, who reported to Henry Wright, who reported in turn to Sir Thomas Challoner who worked under the general direction of the Chief Justice (Popham). It is to be assumed that Davies was not the only 'discoverer' and that he and his like would each have a circle of informers and contacts. And where, it would be fair to ask, would their researches begin? Obviously they would set a watch on the known suspects, the men with a record and, above all, the men who played a part in the Essex Rebellion; the Essexians as they were called. When the Babington Plot was being planned (see page 18), twelve or fourteen young men were in the habit of supping together. Noticing this, the government spies bribed the servant of one of them. Then there was panic and one of them betrayed the rest. It is to be assumed that Salisbury took all the reasonable and by now traditional precautions. The suspects would all be under occasional surveillance. Who was supping with whom? Nor would these routine inquiries be confined to London. Recusants were more numerous in certain parts of England; in Hereford, for example, and in parts of Yorkshire and Lancashire. We must suppose that the 'discoverers' were discreetly active in these parts, asking innocent questions, posing as Catholics, watching certain houses, noting the movements of certain people. The existence of a plot would be sensed long before its nature could be known.

Other precautions were not quite so obvious. To encourage disunity among the Catholics themselves it was advisable to have some known Catholics or Catholic sympathizers in the government itself. These were the tame ducks used as decoys for the wild ones. Chief among them were the Howards; the Earl of Nottingham (the Lord Admiral); the Earl of Suffolk (Lord Chamberlain); the Earl of Northampton (Warden of the Cinque Ports). The Earl of Northampton was a Catholic and an Essexian but had been forgiven. Nottingham was a Protestant but popularly supposed to be a Catholic, and the same could be said of Suffolk. Similar favour was shown to Thomas Arundell, who received a peerage as Lord Arundell of Wardour. But the key figure in this category was Lord Mounteagle who had been a Catholic but professed to have become a Protestant. On the occasion of a Star Chamber trial in 1604 Dr Bancroft, the Archbishop of Canterbury, remarked significantly that nothing was to be discovered about the Catholics 'but by putting some Judas amongst them'. He thus gave casual expression to what was in fact the government policy; and is indeed the policy of any government faced by any sort of conspiracy. Had the conspirators been known by name the plan would have been, and eventually was, to add another name to the list, that of a government spy. In the meanwhile, however, and before anything much more was known, a useful move would be to brief a more equivocal Judas, the sort of man the conspirators would inevitably meet, a man perhaps in whom they might possibly confide. For this role the Lord Mounteagle was ideal as the facts of his career will serve to indicate. From what we know about him it is clear that no better choice could have been made.

William Parker (1575–1622) was the grandson of a well-known and reputedly dangerous recusant, the 9th Baron Morley, who left England in about 1569 and lived abroad thereafter under Spanish protection, a traitor to his country. What made his reputation worse was the fact that he was a descendant of Robert de Morley who commanded at the victorious battle of Sluys in 1340. Henry Parker, the 8th Baron, remained a devoted Catholic under Henry VIII and was related to most of the other leading Catholic families. He married a descendant of Edward Stanley, the 1st Baron Mounteagle (1460?–1523) who was a son of the 1st Earl of Derby and was also notably devout. Of William's father the 10th Baron, the salient fact is that he survived almost long enough to outlive his successor in the title. So William was for much of his life a man of great expectations combining potential power with present (relative) poverty. His only possible remedy was to marry an heiress but in this he was not entirely successful. When aged only seventeen, he married Elizabeth, daughter of Sir Thomas Tresham, a wealthy recusant who was imprisoned for seven years for harbouring the Jesuit Edmund Campion. Unfortunately Sir Thomas also had a son, Francis Tresham, who would eventually be his heir. It is probable, indeed, that Parker and Tresham had been at Oxford together, and that this was how Parker came to meet his future wife. Mrs William Parker brought with her a property at Hoxton, just outside London. This never became his principal residence, however, for his country house was at Great Hallingbury, near Bishop Stortford, and his town house seems to have been in the Strand. She had no great fortune otherwise and young Parker was merely one of the young men at court. When the Earl of Essex staged his rebellion, the last phase of his conflict with the Cecils, young Parker was on the losing side but escaped with a fine which his family could ill afford. Until about 1602 his recusant background was impeccable. Then he changed sides and petitioned for a summons to sit in the House of Lords with a title derived from his mother's family. There was nothing automatic about this claim and he was lucky to become Lord Mounteagle. He could claim, however, that he and Lord Southampton had held the Tower of London for the king during the days which followed the old queen's death. At about the same time he assured the king that he had become, or would become, a Protestant. 'I was breed up,' he wrote, 'in the Romish religion and walked in that because I knew no better, so have I not sodainly or lightly made the change, which now I desire to be seane in . . . Not gain, nor honor, no not that which I doe most highly valew, your majestie's favour, or better opinion of me' [is my motive].

How real and how public his conversion was, must remain in doubt but he evidently continued to move among his Catholic friends and passed as one of them. His change of heart had been abrupt. Lucky to escape execution in 1601 he had become one of the establishment by 1605. But how had he worked his passage? To have that peerage revived for him and to be received into favour, these were no ordinary concessions. How did he come to deserve them? What had he to offer? All he could do in return for favours received was to keep a close watch on his Catholic contemporaries and report any activities which looked suspicious. There can be little doubt that this was his function but we cannot expect documentary proof for none would ever have existed. Whatever understanding he had with the Earl of Salisbury would be verbal and secret. Had he any knowledge of the other spies or discoverers, the seedy characters who moved among the grooms and chambermaids? Most probably not. Information came to Salisbury on different levels and it was for him to piece it together. There is reason to suppose that he had a gift for this. We may fairly conclude that he had his wits about him.

Mounteagle, as he was now to become, did not rely wholly on his own lines of innocent inquiry. He had his own gentlemen, and chief among them was Mr Thomas Ward, his secretary and probably his cousin. If we may accept the opinion of Mr H.H. Spink, Ward was of Mulwith, a brother of Marmaduke Ward, and probably aged about forty-six, an older man than his employer and one who had gained some experience of diplomacy. Ward, of whom we know little, was evidently a man on whom Mounteagle could depend, even perhaps in matters that were highly confidential. He had other followers, however, and one of them was Thomas Winter or Wintour. Of him we know a great deal more. He came of a Worcestershire family and his mother was the daughter of Sir William Ingleby of Ripley Castle, near Knaresborough. An uncle of Thomas had been a Catholic priest and was executed at York. Thomas was a soldier who had seen active service in Flanders and elsewhere and he would appear to have been unmarried. He was fluent in several languages and it was said of him at the time that:

... he was of such a wit and so fine a carriage, that he was of so pleasing conversation, desired much of the better sort ... He was of mean stature but strong and comely and very valiant; about thirty-three years old, or somewhat more. His means were not great, but he lived in good sort, and with the best.[6]

What is not apparent is the office he held in Mounteagle's household. He might have been steward with only occasional duties such as rent collecting. He had not been involved in the Essex Rebellion, probably because he was overseas at the time. He had actually fought on the Dutch side in Flanders, which suggests that he had not always been as fervent a Catholic as we know him to have become.

In so far as Mounteagle was working for the government, atoning for past misdeeds, proving his loyalty and usefulness, it becomes a question whether his gentlemen were aware of the fact. The answer would seem to be that Ward knew all about it and Winter did not. Ward it was who did the confidential work and it would have been difficult to keep him in ignorance about Mounteagle's special relationship with the Earl of Salisbury. Winter's function was quite different, we may suspect, and he would have had religious scruples about assisting Mounteagle in counter-espionage. Ward, by contrast, may well have been a Protestant and the same could no doubt be said of that still more obscure figure, Marmaduke Ward, who was probably his brother. For all we know, incidentally, Mounteagle may have had other assistants in his work.

In the chapters which follow we shall be studying conspiracy and we may have prepared ourselves mentally for a story on two levels. On the higher level we may expect to see royal and noble characters going about their business and pleasure, heedless of impending danger. On the lower level we might expect to see sinister figures meeting in dark cellars, whispering the password and flourishing their cloaks and daggers. It was not, however, that sort of conspiracy. Quite typically, the cellar we shall have occasion to describe was on the ground floor. As for the plotters, they were moving in the best society and chatting easily with the men whose destruction they had planned. The murderers and their intended victims were mostly on the best of terms, attended the same parties and saw each other every week. We assume that the conspirators were always conspiring but the truth is that they mingled with their friends in the ordinary way, some of their social engagements having no significance at all. There is reason to suppose that Thomas Ward and Thomas Winter were on opposite sides but they clearly knew each other extremely well. As for Mounteagle, we can be sure that he made friends easily and especially with those he had come to suspect. As in *Macbeth*, all was politeness until the moment came for the deed. When the king visited Oxford on 27 August 1605, St John's College was foremost in offering entertainment:

Youths in habit and attire like nymphs or sibyls confronted the King, saluting him and putting him in mind of that ancient prophecy made unto Banquo, his majesty's ancestor, that though the sceptre should not come to him yet it should be for ever with his posterity.

The legend of Macbeth seems to have been much in people's minds before the play was actually performed. It is a story which turns, remember, on the murder of a Scottish king.

4

The Church Militant

ROBERT CATESBY was born in 1573, being son and heir to Sir William Catesby of Lapworth in Warwickshire, a man of 'ancient, historic and distinguished lineage' who in about 1580 had been converted to Catholicism by the Jesuits Parsons and Campion. Lady Catesby was the daughter of Sir Robert Throckmorton of Coughton and came thus of a recusant family. Robert was at Gloucester Hall (now Worcester College) Oxford and gained there and in London a reputation for wild behaviour and dissolute extravagance. No religious enthusiast at that time and probably not even a Catholic, he married Catherine Leigh in 1592, she being the daughter of a wealthy Protestant, Sir Thomas Leigh of Stoneleigh in Warwickshire. Before Sir William died in 1598, Robert had inherited from his grandmother an estate at Chastleton in Oxfordshire, but the dowager Lady Catesby retained a life interest in most of her late husband's property. His father's death seems to have brought Robert back to Catholicism and now with fanatical fervour. He took part in the Earl of Essex's rebellion in 1601, was wounded and taken prisoner. With him in this affair were his friends William Parker (Lord Mounteagle), Thomas Percy, John Wright, Francis Tresham and John Grant. Catesby, who had been conspicuous in the riot, was lucky to escape with his life. In order to pay a fine of £3,000 he had to sell his Chastleton estate in 1602. His wife dying at about this time, he went to live with his mother, the dowager Lady Catesby, at Ashby St Leger in Northamptonshire.

Catesby was a good-looking man, six feet tall, athletic and a good

44

swordsman. He had been very wild 'and as he kept company with the best noblemen of the land, so he spent much above his rate, and so wasted also good part of his living'. His manners were attractive and he was said to be generous towards his friends. His chief characteristic lay in his powers of persuasion, which must have been exceptional. He was a natural leader, able to talk his followers into anything. He was always more or less in debt. In modern terms we should picture him as the driver of a dashing sports car, well dressed in a casual way, always ready with a good tip for Ascot or on the stock exchange, willing to take risks and quite unreliable where money is concerned. And yet he was ready to give his life for his faith? It was not, perhaps, as simple as that. We have at least three assessments to choose from. By accepted tradition he and his friends were bloodthirsty scoundrels. By Catholic propaganda they were saintly martyrs for the faith. By another account they were seedy adventurers each ready to betray the others. There is some truth, perhaps, in each of these theories, for human motives can be very confused. We do well, however, to remember that their failure, of which we know in advance, was not inevitable to them. They could dream of a future England in which they would hold office, one as Lord Chancellor and another as Secretary of State. With other motives may have mingled a proportion of ordinary ambition and even avarice.

Spared after the Essex Rebellion (but with that treason certainly not forgotten), Catesby's next thought centred upon an appeal to Spain. Early in 1603 he and William Parker, with Thomas Percy, planned a mission to Madrid. Thomas Winter went as their emissary to Flanders first and so to Spain. There followed Christopher Wright and Guy Fawkes. Their object was to convince the king of Spain that a new invasion attempt would have ample support in England and that the Catholics would readily supply the horses which the invading army might lack. A desultory negotiation followed but it became apparent that the king of Spain had no warlike plans and was intent only on making peace with James 1. The English Catholics, coming to realize this, hoped that a clause about their better treatment might be inserted in the peace treaty. But the

Spanish, profuse in their general expressions of sympathy, would not insist upon any such stipulation. Peace was their object and the conclusion of the treaty meant, for the English Catholics, the end of all their hopes centred upon foreign intervention. Their only remaining chance lay in Elizabeth being succeeded by a more tolerant monarch. For a moment it had looked as if James would be just such a king. When that hope too was at an end, Robert Catesby decided on a more drastic course of action. Early in 1604, during Lent, he asked Thomas Winter to come up to London and visit him at his house at Lambeth. Winter finally did so and found Catesby there with John Wright, another old friend and another Catholic who had been active in Essex's Rebellion.

At the first meeting Catesby told the other two that he had thought of a way to deliver the Catholics and, without foreign help, re-establish Catholicism in England. His plan was to blow up the House of Lords with gunpowder on the day and at the hour when Parliament met. The explosion would kill the king and queen, their children and other members of the royal family, the peers of the realm, the judges, the leading lawyers and the members of the House of Commons. It would also – though he did not stress the point – kill several foreign ambassadors. Winter was startled but had to admit that the plan struck at the root. But what if it failed? How would that affect the future of Catholicism in England? Catesby replied that the nature of the disease required a sharp remedy. Winter now emphasized the practical difficulties but Catesby brushed these aside, saying, 'Let us give the attempt and where it faileth, pass no further.' Winter agreed to join with Catesby but there is no record of what John Wright had to say, possibly because he had already yielded to Catesby's persuasion. John Wright came of a good Yorkshire family settled at Plowland Hall in Holderness but was himself living at Twigmore in Lincolnshire. He was said to be one of the best swordsmen of his time and had been with Catesby in the Essex Rebellion. Catesby now proposed that Winter should go over to the Netherlands and make a last appeal to the Constable of Castile who was on his way to conclude the peace treaty in England. That this envoy would make any stipulation about the treatment of the English Catholics was most improbable, as Catesby knew, and this object of Winter's mission was merely to satisfy Winter's own scruples. The other and more important object of the mission was to fetch Guy Fawkes, who had already been to Spain on a diplomatic mission with Christopher Wright, John Wright's brother. It was evidently agreed from the outset that Fawkes should be one of the conspirators.

Guy Fawkes was born in 1570, the son of William Fawkes, Registrar and Advocate of the Consistory Court at York. William had married Ellen Harrington, daughter of a former lord mayor of York who had held office in 1536. Guy was christened at the Church of St Michael-le-Belfrey and lived with his parents at a house in Stonegate (see Appendix I) close to York Minster. He was sent to school at the ancient grammar school of St Peter's which had been re-endowed as the Royal School of Philip and Mary and was sited in the Horse Fair, Gilligate, just outside the city walls. The headmaster was the Rev. John Pullen, BA, of Caius College, Cambridge; whose predecessor, John Fletcher, had become a Catholic, for which offence he had been removed and imprisoned by Archbishop Grindal. In 1579, William Fawkes died and his wife, after a decent interval, married Dionys Bainbrigge of Scotton in Nidderdale. Guy may have continued his schooling, now as a boarder, and he clearly became a close friend of the Wright brothers, John and Christopher, who were Catholics and who came from Plowland Hall in Holderness. Francis Ingleby, the priest who was executed in York in 1586, was the Wrights' uncle. A future Jesuit and martyr, Robert Middleton, was another pupil at St Peter's in Guy's time; and Oswald Tesimond or Greenway, also to become a Jesuit, had probably left the school a few years earlier. With his father dead and with Catholic influences around him both at school and at home, Guy was probably a Catholic by the time he reached the age of eighteen.

We know little about Guy Fawkes' life after he left school but he is mentioned in a letter from Lord Montague to the Earl of Dorset:

... he should seem to have been my servant once ... for such a one I had even for some four months, about the time of my marriage, but was dismissed from me by my lord upon some dislike he had of him; and discontinued for a year, till some six months after my lord's death, at what time he coming to one Spencer, that was, as it were, my steward and his kinsman, the same Spencer entreated me, that for that instant (being some few days) he might wait at my table, which he did, and departed, and from that time I never had to do with him, nor scarcely thought of him.[1]

This incident, dating perhaps from about 1591–2, would seem to suggest that Fawkes lived as other young gentlemen did, attached at different times to different noble households. He came of age at this time, however, and inherited a small property in Clifton, outside York, which had belonged to his father. He promptly sold this (1592) with his mother's agreement, for the sum of £29 13s 4d and evidently used the money to equip himself for a military career. He went to the Netherlands and enlisted in the English Regiment under Sir William Stanley. He is said to have been present at the siege of Calais in 1596, as also at the battle of Nieuport. He was certainly wounded and he is believed to have fought gallantly. As against that, he rose to no higher rank than ensign (or second lieutenant) and we hear of him acting as Sir William Stanley's steward and thus working alongside Hugh Owen who was Stanley's intelligence expert. There followed his mission to Spain but he was back in Brussels with Sir William when Thomas Winter came to fetch him. Winter and Fawkes landed in England towards the end of April 1604 to hear that Catesby had enlisted another conspirator, Thomas Percy.

The fateful meeting of the five conspirators took place on 20 May probably at the Duck and Drake in St Clement's parish, off the Strand, where Thomas Winter usually stayed when in London. We already know something of Catesby, Thomas Winter, John Wright and Guy Fawkes. They were very different in character. Catesby was 'a very cunning subtle man, exceedingly entangled in debts and scarce able to subsist', a born leader, flashy, brave, a liar and gambler. Thomas Winter was the soldier among them and one who had reached the rank of captain, arguably the best man in the group. John Wright, usually called Jack Wright, was a simpler character whose sister had married Thomas Percy. It has been suggested that

Guy Fawkes was recruited as a mining expert but all veterans of the war in the Netherlands were more or less familiar with siege warfare; and so were many other people, Shakespeare included:

FLUELLEN ... look ye, the mines is not according to the disciplines of the war; the concavities of it is not sufficient; for, look you, th' athversary — you may discuss unto the Duke, look you — is digt himself four yards under the countermines: by Cheshu, I think a' will plow up all, if there is not better direction. *(Henry V* Act III Scene 3)

Guy Fawkes was a useful man, without doubt, and personally known to Winter, his fellow traveller, and John Wright, his school-fellow. His importance lay, however, in another circumstance. He had been out of England for twelve years and nobody in London knew him by sight. If a mine were to be dug, one of the conspirators must be free to fetch food and ale and he must not be recognized by passers-by. The others were perfectly well known, and known in effect to the police, but Guy could pose as a servant or workman and nobody would notice him.

And now there was added the last member of the five: Thomas Percy. As compared with the others, he was clearly a crook. He has already been mentioned as the representative sent to James in Scotland by the Earl of Northumberland, by whom he was recognized as a cousin. The Earl had appointed him a Gentleman Pensioner and retained him as steward despite the repeated complaints of the tenantry he is supposed to have swindled. He was an older man than the other conspirators, aged about forty-five or forty-six and looked older, and he had a special grudge against the king, believing that he had been duped by him; which indeed was true. He was essential to the Gunpowder Plot because his position at court might allow him to rent one or other of the buildings near the House of Lords from which the tunnel might be dug. He was well known to Catesby, a firm Catholic, resolute in his opposition to the Salisbury administration. What is more doubtful about him is his exact relationship to the Earl of Northumberland but as the Earl regarded him as a cousin we must accept their kinship, however distant, as a fact. With the other four he shared one basic characteristic:

he combined a certain social position with a lack of independent means. His duties as Gentleman Pensioner would not seem to have interfered very much with his other activities. He could evidently spare time to do what had to be done, and it was he who brought that first meeting to order with the words: 'Well, gentlemen, shall we always *talk* and never *do* anything?'

A few days later the same group met again, this time at a house beyond St Clement's Inn and all five took a solemn oath, kneeling, with their hands laid on a primer. The words used were as follows: 'You shall swear by the blessed Trinity, and by the sacrament you now propose to receive, never to disclose directly or indirectly, by word or circumstance, the matter that shall be proposed to you to keep secret, nor desist from the execution thereof until the rest shall give you leave.' The Gunpowder Plot was then explained to Percy and Fawkes, the two who had not been privy to the original discussion. All then adjourned to an upper room in the same house where they heard mass and received the sacrament from Father Gerard, SJ, who had not, however, been admitted to the secret. This oath is important to the story and we can assume that it would not be broken by any of the conspirators. They had their faults, and their intentions can be fairly described as criminal; but they were deeply religious men to whom such an oath, followed by the sacrament, would have been utterly sacred. There were only five of them, moreover, closely linked by friendship and religion, two of them Essexians and two of them schoolfellows. We can assume that the secret would be kept.

How did the team measure up to its task? There was Catesby to lead and inspire, Tom Winter to help decide on what was possible, Percy to exert the necessary influence at court and John Wright, related to Percy and loyal to Catesby. Completing the team was Guy or Guido Fawkes who would be known to Salisbury by name but unknown to anyone by sight. For the work of digging a narrow tunnel, one man in turn could dig, one could remove the soil, one could dispose of it and one could recuperate, leaving the last to mount guard in his character of caretaker or servant. This deployment would vary somewhat as between night and day but the number, as we can see, and as they discovered, was minimal. Five, the ideal number for secrecy, was plainly insufficient for rapid progress. There was, moreover, the question as to what was to happen *after* the explosion. The need was for a body of troops to move in, proclaiming a new monarch. But where were the troops and who was going to lead them? There was no army in England and the only available force was the English regiment serving with the Spanish in the Low Countries, the unit from which Guy Fawkes was on indefinite leave. This force was to be rendered harmless by King James in the cheapest possible way, by the appointment to it as Colonel of Lord Arundell of Wardour: a Catholic who was on James's side. Guy would not have known about this but there was, in any case, the difficulty of bringing it over against Dutch opposition. Next best would be to raise in England a further regiment — say, of cavalry — ostensibly for service with the Spanish, but available in the meanwhile for something more important. This was not impossible and the cover plan was good but it could not be organized by the same people who were digging the mine. Sooner or later, the team of five would have to be reinforced, each further recruit being a security risk. As the five were the best men available to join in the plot, each available man would be a shade less reliable. This was a difficulty that would have to be faced but it was brushed aside, no doubt, in the early stages, Catesby probably assuring the others that each problem would be overcome as they came to it.

How would the team appear to Lord Salisbury if and when he should become aware of the plot? It is clear, first of all, that the plot was exactly what he wanted. The crime proposed was so terrible that its discovery would paralyse the Catholics for at least a generation. It would brand them as regicides, anarchists and murderers. Nothing could have suited him better. This is so manifest that some authors have dared to suggest that Salisbury thought of the plot and suggested it, through an intermediary, to Catesby. There is no proof of this and the facts point, indeed, to a different conclusion. But the plot would be welcome to the Privy Council and the more so in that Percy's part in it could be made to implicate Salisbury's enemy, the Earl of Northumberland; the third opponent whose ruin seemed

essential. It is also important to realize that the plotters were vulnerable from the outset in being known. Catesby had been one of those
arrested when Queen Elizabeth died, not on any particular charge
but merely as a safety precaution. He and his immediate friends
were suspect before they had done anything. They were even more
vulnerable, however, in another way. Lord Mounteagle, like Lord
Arundell, was one of Salisbury's outposts, a man who looked like an
opponent but who was in truth an ally, and Thomas Winter was
actually in Mounteagle's service. Winter was bound by oath but he
and Thomas Ward were close friends. We need not suppose that
Mounteagle would be told all the details but a channel existed
through which he could sense that something was being planned. So
while we follow the course of the conspiracy we can assume that spies
were alert for possible clues and that Mounteagle, casually, meeting
the plotters each week, was observant as well as friendly. How long
would it be before someone as astute as Sir Robert Cecil came to
hear some whisper of a possible conspiracy?

The first move in the plot was the agreement, dated 24 May
1604, by which Thomas Percy acquired from one Ferris the sub-
tenancy of a building adjacent to the Parliament House which was
let in the first instance to Whinniard, the keeper of the king's ward-
robe. A tunnel made from thence would allow the gunpowder to be
placed under the House of Lords. Fawkes was given the keys and
appeared as Percy's servant under the name of John Johnson.
Catesby's house was on the other side of the river at Lambeth and
this would be the rear base at which the timber, tools and gunpowder
might be collected. It at once became apparent that a caretaker at
Lambeth would be needed and one who could not be ignorant of the
plot. The man chosen was the penniless Robert Keyes, whose
mother was daughter of the wealthy recusant Sir Robert Tyrwhitt of
Kettleby in Lincolnshire. Father Greenway says that Keyes 'was
introduced merely for the sake of his personal services, having no
estates . . .' Keyes was a member of the Catholic Lord Mordaunt's
household at Turvey in Bedfordshire in which his wife served as
governess.

Soon afterwards Parliament was adjourned until 7 February 1605

SERO, SED SERIO

1 Robert Cecil, First Earl of Salisbury, who became Secretary of State in 1590.

Milites Provinciarum & Burgenses (quos vocant) utrinq, qui Cameram Parlamenti inferiorem constituunt, Prolocutorem conducentes.

2 OPPOSITE Queen Elizabeth I seated in Parliament.

The religious conflict of Elizabeth's reign was essentially a struggle for power. Amongst the many Catholics executed after the discovery of plots were several eminent aristocrats who were seen as a direct threat to the monarchy:

3 RIGHT The Duke of Norfolk who was executed in 1572 after he took part in the Ridolphi Plot.

4 BELOW The execution of Mary Queen of Scots, 1587, after the discovery of the Babington Plot.

5 BELOW RIGHT The Earl of Essex, at one time a favourite of Elizabeth, who was executed in 1601 after attempting a rebellion.

6 King James VI of Scotland and I of England.

7 A seventeenth-century broadsheet showing Great Britain's deliverance from papist machinations: on the left a storm wrecks the Spanish Armada, on the right Guy Fawkes prepares to blow up Parliament but the eye of God is watching him, and in the centre the Pope conspires with, amongst others, the devil, to ruin Britain on 5 November.

ROBᵗ. CATESBY..
One. of The Conspirators..
in the *GUNPOWDER PLOT*..

8 LEFT Robert Catesby the instigator of the Gunpowder Plot as depicted in a stylized print.

10 OPPOSITE ABOVE The letter of betrayal which was sent to Lord Mounteagle and led to the 'discovery' of the plot.

11 OPPOSITE BELOW A cartoon from Vicars' *Mischeefes Mystery* (1617) showing the deliverance of the Mounteagle letter to Robert Cecil.

9 BELOW The house in Lambeth which the conspirators used as their headquarters.

my lord out of the loue i beare To some of youere frendz
i haue a caer of youer preseruacion therfor i would
aduyse yowe as yowe tender youer lyf to deuyse some
excuse to shift of youer attendance at this parleament
for god and man hathe concurred to punishe the wickednes
of this tyme and thinke not slightlye of this aduertisment
but retere youre self into youre contri wheare yowe
maye expect the euent in safti for thowghe theare be no
apparance of anni stirr yet i saye they shall receyue a terrible
blowe this parleament and yet they shall not seie who
hurts them this councel is not to be contemned becaus
it maye do yowe good and can do yowe no harme for the
dangere is passed as soon as yowe haue burnt the letter
and i hope god will giue yowe the grace to mak good
use of it to whose holy proteccion i comend yowe

To the ryght honorable
the lord mowteagle

The gallant *Eagle*, ſoaring vp on high :
Beares in his beake, *Treaſons* diſcouery.
MOVNT, noble EAGLE, with thy happy prey,
And thy rich *Prize* to th' *King* with ſpeed conuay.

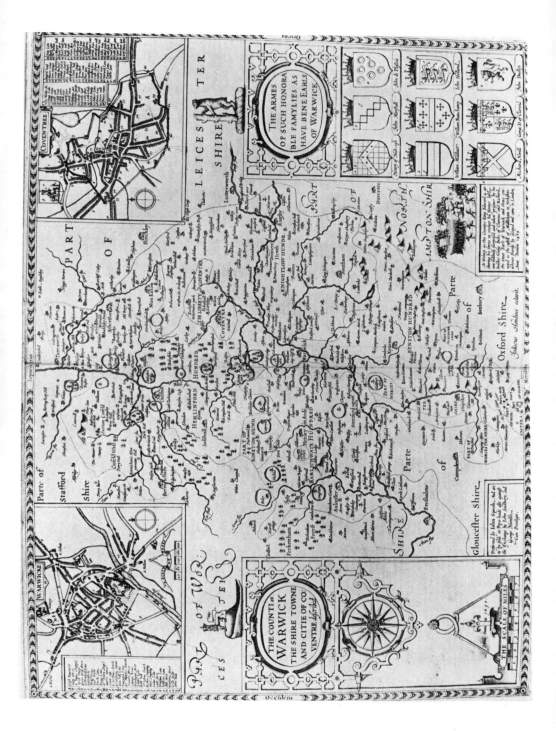

13 The Old Gatehouse of Robert Catesby's home at Ashby St Leger, where the rebels met after Guy Fawkes' arrest.

12 OPPOSITE Speede's Map of Warwick (1610) showing the area in which the rebellion was to take place following the explosion in Westminster.

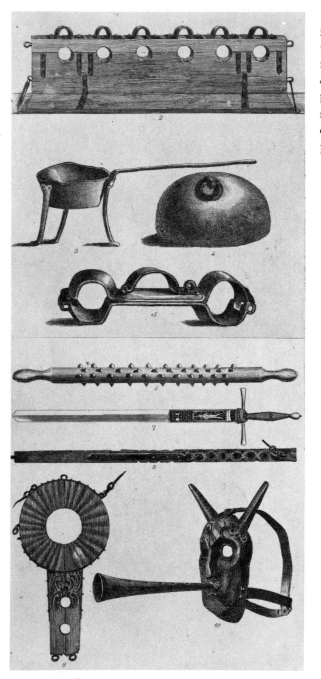

14 LEFT Seventeenth-century instruments of torture, similar to those used to extract confessions from the conspirators. *Top to bottom, left to right*: stocks; pitch pan; stone for pressing; leg manacles; 'larded hare'; executioners' swords; 'violin'; punishment mask.

15 BELOW A pair of thumb-screws, another popular instrument of torture. The major part of prosecution evidence at treason trials of the time was signed confessions extracted after torture

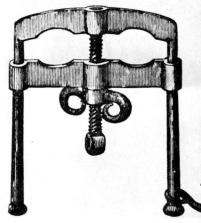

16 Guy Fawkes' lantern.

17 The autographs of Guy Fawkes before and after torture.

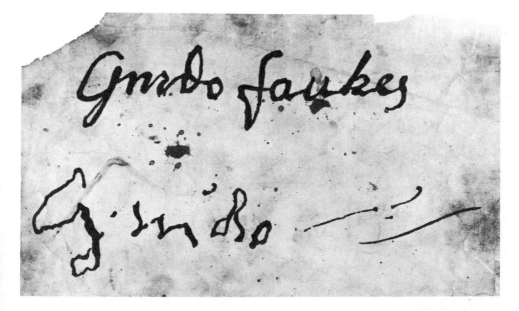

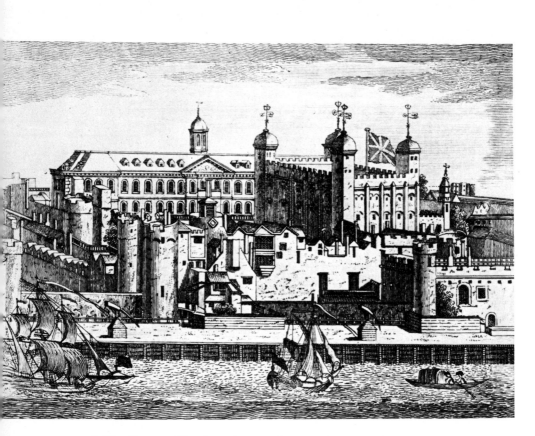

18 The Tower of London where the interrogations took place.

19 A view of Westminster Hall – the scene of the trials.

Sala Regalis cum Curia West-monastery, *vulgo*, Westminster haall.

20 ABOVE A print showing
the execution of the
Gunpowder Conspirators –
they were hanged, drawn
and quartered.

21 LEFT Henry Garnett,
the Jesuit priest, who was
executed on 3 May 1601
after he had been found
guilty of treason in
connection with the
Gunpowder Plot.

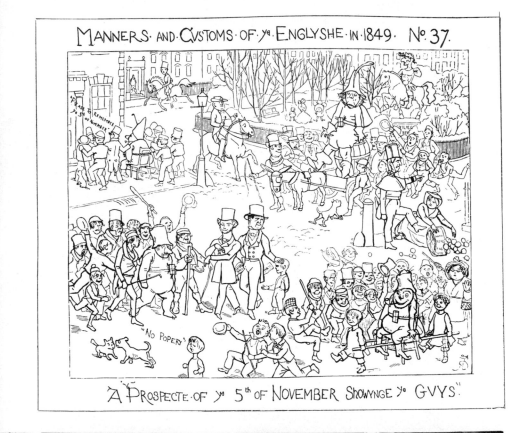

MANNERS·AND·CVSTOMS·OF·yᵉ·ENGLYSHE·IN·1849. Nº.37.

"A PROSPECTE·OF·yᵉ 5ᵗʰ OF NOVEMBER Showynge yᵉ GVYS"

22 OPPOSITE ABOVE A Victorian scene on Guy Fawkes Day – today the celebrations have become far removed from the religious conflict of the seventeenth century but in this picture 'No Popery' is still the cry to accompany the 'Guy'.

24 RIGHT The royal body-guard searching the vaults of the Houses of Parliament, a ritual which has been carried out each year before the opening of the session ever since the Gunpowder Plot.

23 OPPOSITE BELOW An horrific 'Guy' being drawn through the streets in 1877.

25 BELOW Hatfield House, the home which Robert Cecil was given but never saw completed to his taste. It remains a memorial to one of Britain's most successful statesmen.

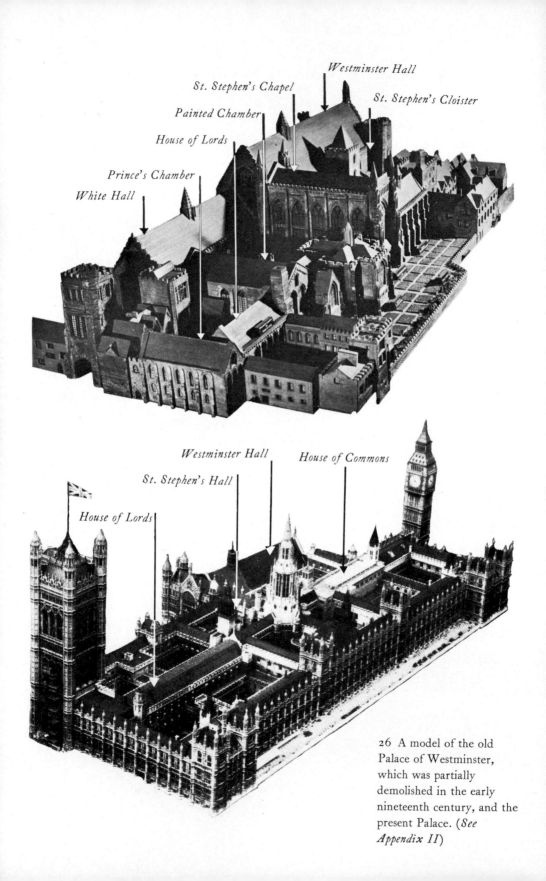

White Hall

Prince's Chamber

House of Lords

Painted Chamber

St. Stephen's Chapel

Westminster Hall

St. Stephen's Cloister

House of Lords

St. Stephen's Hall

Westminster Hall

House of Commons

26 A model of the old Palace of Westminster, which was partially demolished in the early nineteenth century, and the present Palace. (*See Appendix II*)

and the conspirators dispersed, agreeing to assemble again early in December of 1604. The chief events of that summer took place not in the cellar but in the wider field of politics and diplomacy. The royal consent was given to a new Recusancy Act, executions under the Act beginning at Manchester. The Treaty of Peace was set in motion. Fines were collected from the thirteen Catholics rich enough to pay £20 per month. A Mr Pound who petitioned the king for tolerance was brought before the Star Chamber, imprisoned in the Fleet Prison, fined £1,000 and sentenced to stand in the pillory at both Lancaster and Westminster. Pressure on the Catholics was being steadily increased, almost as if the government were forcing them to rebel. Historians have pointed out that the plot was devised before the persecutions began, which is perfectly true, but the plotters were at least given what they must have regarded as further provocation.

At this point in the story some scholars have raised a doubt concerning the availability of gunpowder, much as if it had been like uranium today. They feel that the plotters must have obtained it with government connivance or else that it was never obtained at all. And why, they have asked, were the conspirators not questioned about their sources of supply? The problem raised does not, in fact, exist. There is not, nor has there ever been, any mystery about it. There was gunpowder in plenty and anyone could buy it. Elizabeth had granted a monopoly in 1558 to Richard Hills and George and John Evelyn but this had never extended to London. By 1555 there were powder mills near Rotherhithe, by 1561 near Waltham Abbey. From 1590 George Evelyn (grandfather of the diarist) set up his works at Long Ditton and at Leigh Place near Godstone. There were other mills at Faversham and 'from Redriffe it is reported (1603) that . . . thirteen persons were slain and blown in pieces with gunpowder by misfortune at the gunpowder mill.' Next year there came this report from the siege of Ostend:

They have blown up a mine between the Poulder Bulwark and West Port. A sloop laden with 2000 weight of powder being foul upon entrance of the haven, was struck with a shot and the powder all blown up in the air and fourteen men lost in it.[2]

There was God's plenty of powder, although rather expensive at 8s 2d per pound in 1595. Tons of it were being used in the Low Countries. Every merchant ship of any size would need barrels of it. The militia and trained bands needed it and a fair amount was used on the stage – (A flourish of trumpets, and ordnance shot off, within – *Hamlet*, Act I Scene 4). The plotters are said to have spent £200 on powder, as well they might. But no one then or now need ask where they bought it. They bought the stuff where everyone else did, from the merchants and most probably in London.

On or about 11 December 1604 the plotters assembled again, entering the house late at night with a good supply of hard-boiled eggs, baked meats and pasties. They had first to carry their tunnel up to the wall which formed the foundation of the Parliament House. It turned out to be a harder task than they had expected, the wall itself being a very tough obstacle indeed. They needed reinforcements and obtained them by bringing Keyes over from Lambeth (together with the gunpowder) and enlisting Christopher Wright, John's younger brother. The team now numbered seven:

... All which seven were gentlemen of name and blood; and not any was employed in or about this action (no, not so much as in digging or mining) that was not a gentleman. And while the others wrought, I stood as sentinel to descry any man that came near; and when any man came near to the place, upon warning given by me, they ceased until they had again notice from me to proceed; and we seven lay in the house, and had shot and powder, and we all resolved to die in that place before we yielded or were taken.

Like Fawkes, other commentators were to be impressed by the fact that the work was being done by 'men of their quality, accustomed to live in ease and delicacy'. They worked well but the fact was that they had wasted too much time before they began. To finish their task by 7 February was virtually impossible, as they must have realized. But at this point the government obligingly postponed the meeting of Parliament until 3 October, giving as reason the prevalence of plague in certain counties and the undesirability of bringing the plague to London. The real motive for the prorogation lay in James's plan for a union of England with

Scotland. Whether desirable or premature in itself, this plan involved enormous administrative and legal difficulties and Sir Robert Cecil, now Lord Cranborne, was reluctant to grasp the thistle. If the whole business could be postponed, the king's enthusiasm might dwindle. This action saved the conspiracy and the plotters now had time enough to complete their tunnel and organize the military action which was to follow the big explosion. They dispersed again for Christmas, Gatesby and Percy being authorized by the rest to recruit more conspirators. This they did, holding a meeting at Oxford early in January which was attended by John Grant of Norbrook near Warwick and Robert Winter of Huddington. Grant was a Catholic who had been involved in the Essex Rebellion and was married to a sister of Robert Winter. His house at Norbrook, between Warwick and Stratford-on-Avon, was 'walled and moated, and well calculated, from its great extent, for the reception of horses and ammunition'. He was said to be melancholy and taciturn. Robert Winter was Thomas's elder brother and owned the family estate, had married the daughter of John Talbot of Grafton in Worcestershire and was reluctant at first to join in the plot. One other and very minor conspirator was Thomas Bates, one of Catesby's servants, who had come to suspect what was happening and was put under oath as a safety measure. Late in January the work began again, becoming progressively more difficult, and reached a point where the tunnel began to fill with water. This impeded the work but, more to the point, showed that the whole plan was impossible. Once damp, the powder would be useless. Work continued but one must suppose with dwindling enthusiasm and the conspirators had to face the fact that their scheme had failed. In March Thomas Winter applied for permission to join the English Regiment in the Low Countries. For him, at least, the game was over.

In trying to understand the story of this plot we have to fix, first of all, the approximate date on which the Secretary of State came to hear about it. We know, on the one hand, that the conspirators were active and were adding to their number, with all the security risks that this recruitment would involve. We know, on the other hand,

that the government's detectives – with Wright and Davies report-
ing to Challoner – were as active on their side and could claim afterwards – as they did – that they had discovered some important
information. So they had, no doubt, but the central figure in the
counter-plot would seem to have been Lord Mounteagle. How
much did he discover and when and how? All must be guesswork
but the likelihood is that he knew what was being attempted and,
roughly, by whom. The moment of discovery would be the moment
when the scheme was abandoned, the moment when security had
come to matter less. There had been an oath of secrecy but that
related, after all, to a plan in course of execution. It could not apply
with quite the same force to a merely historical reference to a scheme
that had failed. That Thomas Winter would actually tell Mounteagle
is most improbable but he might have been a little careless or un-
guarded. One wonders, for example, how these gallants accounted
for their blistered and calloused hands? Today we should admit to
having done some gardening over the weekend. But no gentleman
dirtied his hands in those days. And how, again, did these men
account for their periods of absence from their common haunts? Of
this we can be certain, that Tom Winter, the soldier among them,
would have been the first to see that their mine was a failure. His
reaction was to decide on leaving the country. His employer,
Mounteagle, would have asked him why. What would his answer
have been? Or was it Thomas Ward who asked the question? Winter
we can be sure, would never have knowingly betrayed his friends
but could he not have drunk too much in his moment of frustration?
Two words, perhaps, used indirectly 'in circumlocution' and 'afar
off', would have been enough; 'gunpowder' and 'Parliament'. Given
so much, Mounteagle would have gone at once to the Secretary of
State. There had been a plot to blow up Parliament but it was
coming to nothing, the tunnel had proved too wet to use, as was
likely enough so close to the river. Tom Winter had been involved
but he was planning to leave the country. What more need Mounteagle have said? It remained for the Secretary of State to collate this
with other information received and then ask about the tenure of
buildings which abutted on the House of Lords. What was sublet to

whom? He would thus have the name of Thomas Percy . . . a cousin of the Earl of Northumberland: just so. And what had Wright and Davies to report? That Catesby, Percy and Winter had often been seen together – yes, with other men too, known recusants and known for their part in the Essex Rebellion? One thing immediately apparent was that the plot was an ideal one from the Privy Council's point of view. Nothing more horrible could have been devised! There could be no doubt, of course, that the Earl of Northumberland was behind it – with, of course, the Jesuits. There might be no evidence against the Jesuits as yet but their guilt could be fairly assumed. And the plot had *failed*! Well – could nothing be done to revive it? It was, frankly, too good a plot to waste.

In counter-espionage work, it is essential from the outset to put yourself in the enemy's position. Sir Robert Cecil, Lord Cranborne, was the last person to ignore this principle. Before Mounteagle had finished talking, the Secretary of State would have asked himself 'How should *I* blow up the House of Lords?' He would at once have dismissed all this nonsense about digging a mine. To obtain the best results the powder would have to be in that ground-floor storage room immediately under the Chamber. Whoever was tenant must be made to surrender his lease and remove all his clutter, whatever it was, and leave the space vacant. Thomas Percy would apply for the tenancy which, after some show of reluctance, would be conceded to him. That would revive the plot, which would be exposed at the very last moment before Parliament met. Timing would be vital. In the meanwhile he would want to complete a list of the conspirators. But wait a minute – what did they mean to do after the explosion? They could not just leave it at that and go home satisfied. The idiots must have some further imbecile plan. They must collect some forces somewhere. Where did Catesby come from? Northamptonshire? And Thomas Winter? His elder brother's estate was somewhere in the midlands. Where did all these recusants live? A list should be made and their places of residence marked on the map. Where would they collect their forces, supposing them to have any? Yorkshire? Too far off. Herefordshire? Too far again. Some inquiries should be made, and the problem was a simple one.

The conspirators were soon delighted to find that the vault beneath the House of Lords was vacant. Percy obtained the tenancy and it only remained to bring in the gunpowder at night and cover the barrels with a load of firewood. This was done in May 1605, and the conspirators then dispersed, agreeing to meet again in September. Fawkes went to Flanders so as to report to Stanley and Owen and in early September Sir Edmund Baynham went to inform the pope. There was no other conspiratorial activity in London until the autumn, but Catesby had now to organize his forces in the midlands. There is reason to suppose that Robert Cecil, now Earl of Salisbury, watched his efforts from afar with a benevolent eye.

5

The Letter

THE area upon which Catesby sought to base his rebellion would mostly fall within a thirty-mile radius of Warwick and would include Worcester, Droitwich, Stratford-on-Avon, Coventry and Rugby; parts, in fact, of Worcestershire, Warwickshire, Northamptonshire and Leicestershire. It would be quite wrong to regard this as the heart of Catholic England but it was a central area of Jesuit activity and the region where Catesby's friends were mostly to be found (see map, No. 12). Henry Garnet, the Jesuit Provincial, was often at Hinlip, the Habington house near Worcester. Catesby himself lived at Ashby St Leger and Robert Winter at Huddington near Droitwich. Considered as a base of operations, not too distant from London, what this area chiefly lacked was a Catholic nobleman of wealth and influence; someone comparable with the Earl of Northumberland. What it possessed, however, was a possible heiress to the throne; the Princess Elizabeth (aged nine), living under the guardianship of Lord Harrington near Coventry. Supposing that the Princes Henry and Charles were to perish with the king and queen, the Princess Elizabeth would be next in succession and would head, theoretically, the march on London. In this and in other respects, the south midlands would serve Catesby's purpose very well. What he needed was a regiment of cavalry which implied, in turn, a great deal of money. All going well, he had a reasonable chance of success.

A reasonable chance is not, however, a certainty. Jacobean England was not as appallingly over-centralized and vulnerable as the England of 1976. With Whitehall and Westminster taken out, there remained some other authorities. There was the Council of the North and the Council of Wales. The Lord Mayor of London had, in effect, an army of his own. There was a Lord Deputy in Ireland with further troops available. So all depended on the speed of the follow-up. The thunder of the explosion should be succeeded at once by the proclamation at Charing Cross of the new Queen Elizabeth. News should follow of her approach through Buckinghamshire and her troops should be in Whitehall within three days. Success on these lines was not impossible but the conspirators were sadly lack ing in practical ability and political sense. Catesby had no military background and Tom Winter's experience was at a company com- mander's level. To organize the march on the capital and set up a new government would seem, on the face of it, to require qualities which the conspirators had never possessed. It was necessary, there- fore, to widen the circle, bringing in men of higher status and greater wealth. The original five, Catesby, Thomas Winter, John Wright, Thomas Percy and Guy Fawkes, were all relatively poor men. The next recruits, to help in the digging, Robert Keyes and Christopher Wright, were, if anything, poorer still; and Bates was only a servant. Those now to be recruited were to be men of the midlands, esquires and men of substance. John Grant, already mentioned, was the first of them and Robert Winter the second. They were quite distinct from the original group and they had no occasion to know who the London conspirators might be. They were to be the nucleus of an army, but the raising of even a small army is not very consistent with secrecy. So there had to be a cover plan and this was provided by the war in the Netherlands:

For this purpose, horses, arms, powder and other ammunition were pur- chased and distributed in the houses of various conspirators in the midland counties, but principally at his own house at Ashby St Leger, and at that of John Grant at Norbrook. This could not be done secretly; and therefore to give colour to these warlike preparations, Catesby took great pains to inform all his friends and acquaintance that he was about to raise a troop of three hundred horse, under the levies which the Spanish Ambassador was then making, and to engage with them in the service of the Archduke in Flanders.

Upon this, many enterprising and discontented gentlemen offered to join him as volunteers, and to advance money and horses for the undertaking.[1]

Having both an ostensible and a real purpose, Catesby had to tell different stories to different people. This was second nature to him and he was finally able to list a fair number of supporters, some eager to sail for the Low Countries, some ready to provide horses and others likely to prove helpful after the explosion had taken place. Those who actually joined the conspiracy, taking the oath as the rest had done, were five, including Grant and Robert Winter. Catesby made careful inquiries beforehand and delayed their formal admission until the autumn. He and Percy met first in Bath and agreed there to approach Sir Everard Digby, Ambrose Rookwood and (after some hesitation) Francis Tresham. Born in 1581, Digby succeeded in childhood to his father's estates of Tilton and Drystoke in Rutlandshire. In 1596 he married an heiress whose parents promptly died, leaving him with another large estate in Buckinghamshire. Digby was a cultivated and accomplished man who had been at court, a keen musician and sportsman, a landowner very generally liked and admired. His weakness lay in the fact that he was aged only twenty-four, was immature and much under Jesuit influence. He provided a good or goodish figurehead for the nucleus army but had no military experience at all. As soon as he had been assured by Catesby (who was lying) that the enterprise had been approved by the Church, he took the oath and agreed to contribute £1,500 in money, together with horses, arms and ammunition. Ambrose Rookwood of Coldham Hall, Suffolk, was another wealthy Catholic, who had married a daughter of Sir William Tyrwhitt of Kettleby in Lincolnshire. He was chiefly known as a horse-breeder and had known Catesby since childhood. His own house was rather remote from the scene of the intended action but he now removed with his family to a house he rented at Clopton, near Stratford-on-Avon. Sir Everard Digby made a similar move from Goathurst (or Gayhurst) where he normally lived, to Coughton, a house near Stratford-on-Avon which belonged to Thomas Throckmorton. The third man of wealth was Francis Tresham, son and heir of the recusant Sir Thomas Tresham who died during the summer of 1605, leaving Francis a rich man; one who had been lucky, however, to escape with a fine after the Essex Rebellion in which he had been conspicuous. Tresham was known to be mean, treacherous and unprincipled but he offered to contribute £2,000, was closely related to Catesby and was perhaps his contemporary at Oxford. At this time, Catesby also had contact with Stephen Littleton, whose house was at Holbeach, four miles from Stourbridge on the road to Wolverhampton. He had a cousin, Humphrey, who would seem to have been a neighbour. Catesby decided eventually against admitting the Littletons to the plot but Stephen was to have been an officer in the force destined in theory for Flanders. The final arrangement was for all the midland group – conspirators, volunteers for service overseas and quite a few Catholics who knew nothing of either scheme – to meet at Dunchurch in Warwickshire; the details to be arranged nearer the time. The convenience of Dunchurch lay in its proximity to Lord Harrington's house near Coventry, but Dunsmoor Heath was also a plausible rendezvous for hunting; and some of those invited would be expecting nothing else.

As the date approached for the meeting of Parliament, Catesby moved nearer to London bringing Sir Everard Digby with him and resuming contact with the original five. The meetings were held at White Webbs in Essex, a rendezvous near London which belonged to Anne Vaux and was much used by Garnet and the other Jesuits. It was agreed, first of all, that Fawkes should be the man to fire the mine. This was an inevitable choice because he was the known caretaker, familiar to the neighbours: a stranger or, worse, a known Catholic gentleman, would have been noticed. He would use a slow-burning match, it was decided, giving him a quarter of an hour in which to escape. He was then to board a ship in the river, chartered in advance, which would take him to Flanders. There followed an argument about the possibility of warning Catholics against attending the opening of Parliament. Tresham urged that a warning should be given to Lords Stourton and Mounteagle, his two brothers-in-law. Robert Keyes wished to warn his patron, Lord Mordaunt, and Guy Fawkes wanted to save his former employer,

Lord Montague. Agreeing about Mounteagle, Percy then put in a word for his employer, the Earl of Northumberland. Others present spoke up for young Lord Arundell. But Catesby and Thomas Winter thought it extremely dangerous to warn anybody. Catesby regarded the noblemen as atheists, fools and cowards, no loss to anyone. Finding, however, that this view was not generally accepted, he quickly changed his tactics, assuring the others that he had already persuaded Lord Montague to stay away and that Lords Mordaunt and Stourton would not be there anyway. It was agreed that no warnings should be given but that some of them might suggest to their friends in the House that their attendance, as a small minority, was a waste of time.

In this instance we know what Catesby had said to Lord Montague because the latter revealed it afterwards to the Earl of Dorset:

... I did lately call to mind, that upon the Tuesday before All Saints Day, in the Savoy, I met Mr Robert Catesby, with whom I had some few words of compliment, and among the rest in these words, or the like: 'The parliament, I think, brings your lordship up now?' Whereunto I answered to this effect and in these words as nigh as I can remember. 'No, surely, but it will on Monday next, unless my Lord Treasurer (Dorset) do obtain me His Majesty's licence to be absent, which I am in some hope of.' Then he said to this effect, 'I think your lordship takes no great pleasure there,' whereunto I assented. And so after a word or two ... I parted from him.[2]

Painstakingly accurate, Montague corrected this letter on the following day, explaining that it must have been the Tuesday *fortnight* before All Saints Day, i.e. 15 October. The point is, however, that Catesby, while lying, was not entirely untruthful. He was that sort of liar.

This little story may serve to remind us that social life was continuing at the same time. People met each other in the street, visited the swordsmith's or saddler's, went to dine with their grandmothers at the Savoy (not then a hotel) or met for supper at some fashionable tavern. Then there was the society wedding (28 December 1604) of Lord Salisbury's niece, Lady Susan Vere, with Philip Herbert, who then became Earl of Montgomery. The king was present and almost rubbed shoulders with Guy Fawkes, smartly dressed and wearing his sword. There was a party on 9 October with Lord Mordaunt and Sir Jocelyn Percy, Winter, Tresham and Ben Jonson, the poet. At another supper party on the 23rd, there was a rather similar group with John Wright in place of Tresham. On the 24th, next day, there was a larger party at the Mitre Tavern in Bread Street with Sir William Monson, the seaman, and Richard Hakluyt, the geographer and historian. There must have been other parties of which we have no record, with Will Shakespeare (for all we know) among those present. One person we often encounter on these social occasions is Lord Mounteagle. On some rather earlier date in 1605 he was, for example, at Fremland, near Downham in Essex, a place much frequented by the Catholics. Garnet, the Jesuit Provincial, found Catesby there together with Mounteagle and Tresham. Suspecting that a plot was hatching, Garnet warned Catesby against 'rushing headlong into mischief' and told him that the Pope was totally opposed to violence. Garnet, by his own account, implored Mounteagle and Tresham to be precise about their intentions:

I asked what they thought of the force of Catholics, whether they were able to make their part good by arms against the King My Lord Mounteagle answered, if ever they were, they were able now, and then added the reason: 'the King (saith he) is so odious to all sorts'.[3]

Tresham assured Garnet that there was no immediate plot but he went further in trying to restrain them: 'No," said I, "assure yourselves they [foreign princes] will do nothing. "What," said my Lord Mounteagle, "will not the Spanish help us? It is a shame." '

In reading this account we should remember that Garnet was a wanted man, someone the authorities had been hunting for twenty years, and that Mounteagle was a peer of the realm and a member, most probably, of the queen's household. Apart from that, we should notice the ease with which Mounteagle moved among his Catholic friends. Garnet assumed that he must be a party to the plot of which Catesby and Tresham denied the existence. Mounteagle was no sworn adherent but could he have moved in that circle

64

without being aware of what was happening? His words as quoted may seem naive; but the part he played was anything but that.

Mounteagle kept the Earl of Salisbury fully informed and the Earl had every reason to look on the plot with quiet satisfaction. He knew about the vault and the gunpowder – the vault had been his own contribution – and he had, from Mounteagle, an incomplete list of the conspirators, lacking the names of Digby, Tresham, Keyes and Bates. He knew about the intended rising in the midlands and was careful to brief the sheriffs of the counties involved. He had, we may suppose, a particularly long session with Sir Richard Walsh, the Sheriff of Worcestershire. He sent at least one government spy to join the revolt, Marmaduke Ward, probably Thomas Ward's brother. From the Earl's point of view the plot was especially convenient in that its climax must come on the day Parliament met, a date and hour to be chosen by the Earl himself. The pity was that there was no evidence as yet to implicate the Jesuits. Garnet he could have arrested at any time but it would of course be better to make his arrest a sequel to the planned rebellion. All the evidence needed would then come from the people who would be questioned, from the servants, pages and grooms. In matters of this sort the Earl of Salisbury was a perfectionist, an artist, a man who saw each operation as a neat, dovetailed device. In this instance the plot's perfection required an aspect which would force the king to see it as his own property. Before the curtain fell on the grand finale the spotlight must be turned on the king while the Secretary of State moved aside with becoming modesty. It must be a repeat, in effect, of the Gowrie Conspiracy, foiled on King James's lucky day. But, wait a minute, the king's day was Tuesday the 5th ... and 5 November would be a Tuesday. So the date must be changed again and Parliament must meet on 5 November rather than 3 October. The date was important but something else must be done to give the king a personal interest. He must somehow be given the credit for discovering the plot. And who more likely than a man whose father had been (well, almost) blown up by gunpowder? He could hardly be lured into conducting the search in person but there could be a document – a letter, say – which would puzzle his ministers but would be understood by him . . . Yes, it should be, on the whole, an anonymous letter – 'Beware the Ides of March'. (Where had he heard that? In some stage play?) And addressed to whom? Why, to Mounteagle, of course. He already knew the whole story. Why reveal all to anyone else? Here would be a secret known to two (no – three) and there was every reason against giving it a wider circulation. In its way this plot was going to be a masterpiece.

The Earl of Salisbury could afford to take his time but the prorogation of Parliament from 7 February until 3 October 1605 put a considerable strain on the conspirators' patience. It gave them time to organize a rising in the midlands, which could not otherwise have taken place at all, but it was a long time to wait for those who had nothing to do with that planned revolt. Guy Fawkes had been given a task to perform, a more or less futile mission to the Low Countries, but Thomas Percy had merely to wait. It is difficult to say at what point his nerve failed him but the moment could have been when Parliament was prorogued yet again to 5 November. We know that several conspirators were alarmed at this time, thinking that the plot had been discovered, as indeed it had, and we also know that Thomas Winter reassured them. The ceremony of prorogation took place with proper form and one of the Commissioners to make the announcement was Lord Mounteagle. Thomas Winter was one of the gentlemen in attendance with him. There were no signs of alarm, he reported, Lord Salisbury moving cheerfully among the other peers, greeting all of them with a word here and there. He did this, remember, in the knowledge that there were thirty-six barrels of gunpowder beneath his feet. But the risk of accident was small and the plotters were as anxious to prevent it, on that day, as he could have been. Salisbury's nerves were steady but Thomas Percy's were not. He decided to reveal the whole plot and bargain for his life. His plan went beyond this, however, for he had seen his way to make a fortune at the same time. It was his task to collect the Earl of Northumberland's quarterly rents and he had already promised to use the money in furtherance of the plot. He realized now that his better plan would be to pocket the whole sum (something under £4,000) and leave the country with all convenient speed. On the

66

sum filched, the equivalent perhaps of £150,000 in today's devalued currency, he could retire in reasonable comfort.

Is Percy's treachery a matter of guesswork or of fact? Our witness here is Dr Godfrey Goodman, the Bishop of Gloucester, who writes:

> I will name my author, who is beyond all exception, Sir Francis Moore, who had been an ancient acquaintance of this Mr. Percy, for he (Moore) had formerly solicited the Earl of Northumberland's suits, and had married his wife out of that house. Being the Lord Keeper Egerton's favourite, and having some occasion of business with him at twelve of the clock at night and going then homeward from York House to the Middle Temple at two, several times he met Mr. Percy coming out of that great statesman's house (i.e. Salisbury's house) and wondered what his business should be there.[4]

Francis Moore, barrister of the Middle Temple and destined for knighthood in 1616, was respectability itself and his evidence must be accepted. It is particularly interesting, moreoever, that this chance meeting happened more than once. If the plot was to be revealed it could be done in a word. The only argument could be over the price but on this question Salisbury, who knew all about it already, had only to say 'No'. Why was Percy told to come back tomorrow or next week?

The truth must be that Percy's confession was most inopportune. The plot was to be revealed on the day when Parliament met, on 5 November, on the king's lucky day. No more dramatic scene could have been planned. And now one of the conspirators wants to betray the rest about a month too soon! What was Salisbury to do about it? It may be questionable, first of all, whether Percy saw the Secretary of State at all. His first interview would have been with an underling and a guarded message would have been carried in. Thomas Percy with secret information? For God's sake! Tell him that his lordship is asleep, like most other honest men at this hour. Tell him to come back on Friday. On his return he would be told to make a written statement. He would next be told that his story was untrue, that he was trying to create needless alarm and that a serious view might be taken of his behaviour. He would be well advised to mind his own business. We can only guess at the tactics used but the effect would be to let the conspiracy take its course. It remained for Thomas Percy to decide whether to leave the country next day. Unfortunately for him, however, the Michaelmas rents had still to be collected. He had to oversee the process, have the pack horses loaded under escort and bring the money up to London. He could not even begin his journey north until nearly the end of October and it would be early November before he could return. His situation was miserable. If the plot succeeded his attempted betrayal would most probably become known to Catesby and Winter, who would cut his throat. If the plot failed he would be arrested at once and tried with the rest on a charge of treason. If this was his supposition, however, he was quite wrong. By his double dealing he had at least escaped the gallows, for Salisbury had now given a final order to Sir Richard Walsh — that Thomas Percy should never be taken alive.

It now remained for the Earl of Salisbury to discover the plot in his own way and in his own time. It is just possible that his action was hastened for a few days by Percy's threatened disclosure. He decided anyway to learn about the plot from an anonymous letter, one that he drafted and had someone else copy in a disguised and somewhat illegible hand.

The letter, addressed to the right honourable the Lord Mounteagle, read as follows:

My lord out of the love i beare to some of youer friends i have a caer of your preservacion therefor i would advyse yowe as youe tender youwer lyf to devyse some excuse to shift yower attendance at this parliament for god and man hathe concurred to punishe the wickedness of the tyme and think not slightlye of this advertisement but retyere youre self into yowre contee whence yowe maye expect the event in safti for thowghe theare be no apparence of anni stir yet I saye they shall receyve a terrible blowe this parleament and yet they shall not seie who hurts them this councel is not to be contemned because it maye do yowe good and can do yowe no harme for the dangere is passed as soon as yowe have burnt this letter and I hope god will give yowe the grace to mak good use of it to whose holy proteccion i commend yowe.[5]

This represents the world's original bomb scare. We read it in the knowledge of what it meant and what the sequel was to be. Its meaning was not so obvious at the time and it could easily have been the work of a lunatic. It was carefully and cleverly composed as a puzzle which might be difficult but was not insoluble by someone to whom the idea of a gunpowder plot was more or less familiar. Mounteagle, to whom the letter was addressed, was told when to expect it and what action he was to take. Salisbury decided that the message should reach Mounteagle at his house at Hoxton, not at his lodging in the Strand. As Father Edwards put it, a messenger from Cecil House might have been recognized in central London: 'A place out of London was called for, somewhere remote and carefully isolated from any anticlimactic factors that could detract from the drama of the essential play: it would also leave at a distance anyone who could remember awkward details or ask embarrassing questions.'

On October 24th Cecil wrote to a close friend, Sir Thomas Lake, who was with the King at Royston, asking him to 'let his Majesty know that I dare boldly say no shower nor storm shall mar our harvest, except it should come from the middle region'.[6]

The king must have known already, in general terms, that there was a plot and that Cecil was keeping his eye on it. When in London Mounteagle seems to have lived ordinarily in the Strand or at his house in Montague Close, a part of the dissolved priory of St Mary's Overie in Southwark. He appears to have made little use of this Hoxton dwelling and his servants had to prepare the place at short notice. He announced his intention of having supper there on 26 October, ten days before Parliament would assemble.

At about seven in the evening of the 26th when Mounteagle was at table, the letter was brought to him by one of his pages to whom it had been handed, outside the house, by a stranger he did not recognize in the dark, but who said that the letter was urgent. The probability is that the messenger was Mr Levinus Monck, Lord Salisbury's secretary, who may also have written it. We may assume that he was heavily cloaked, muffled to the ears and with his hat pulled down over his eyes. We might even surmise that he made a circuitous ride, arriving as if from White Webbs (the artistic touch) and riding off as if to return there. The only weak point in the play was the page happening to be outside when the mysterious stranger arrived. This explained, of course, why the messenger was never seen in the light. Lord Mounteagle opened the letter, saw that it had neither date nor signature, and handed it to Mr Thomas Ward, his secretary, who thereupon read it aloud. There were no guests, presumably Mounteagle being alone but attended by his gentlemen and pages. There were witnesses, however, of all that took place:

But no sooner did he conceive the strange contents thereof, although he was somewhat perplexed what construction to make of it . . . yet did he as a most dutifull and loyal subject conclude not to conceal it, whatever might come of it. Whereupon notwithstanding the latenesse and darknesse of the night in that season of the year, he presently repaired to his Majesties palace at Whitehall and there delivered the same to the Earl of Salisbury his majesties principall secretarie.[7]

When Mounteagle arrived, Salisbury was about to go into a late supper with (as it happened) the other members of what we should call the inner cabinet; that is, the Lord Admiral and the Earls of Suffolk, Worcester and Northampton. Having read the letter the Earl of Salisbury told Mounteagle that 'he had done like a discreet nobleman not to conceal a matter of such a nature, whatever the consequence might prove'. He observed that there might well be a conspiracy among the papists, there had been signs of it for three months past. The letter was then shown to the other lords who agreed that it should go to the king. James was hunting, however, at Royston and was not expected back until Thursday, 31 October. Their lordships also agreed that the Lord Chamberlain should search the Parliament buildings but not immediately, so that the traitors 'might not be scared before they had let the matter run on to a full ripeness for discovery'.

When the letter was shown to the king, three days after his return, ministers refrained from voicing any opinion about it:

. . . but only attended to hear his Majesty's own conceit; whom they find in all such occasions not only endowed with the most admirable gifts of piercing conceit, and a solid judgement, that ever was heard of in any age; but accompanied also with a kind of divine power in judging of the nature and consequence of such advertisements.[8]

Completely at a loss, the ministers looked to their king for guidance. He observed that the letter was anonymous and vague . . . (they exchanged glances; amazed at his perception) . . . but that it *did* seem to presage danger to the whole Court of Parliament. The words hinted at . . . (he paused for a moment in thought) . . . some stratagem of fire and powder. (Ministers gasped in horror and astonishment. How could they have failed to see this for themselves?) Perhaps the Earl of Suffolk should direct a search. As for Mounteagle, he had done extremely well, showing himself a loyal subject and a real lover of his country. It might be as well, the king added, for the names to be taken down of all who asked for leave of absence from Parliament. It was after all unlikely that the warning would be given only to one. As Parliament would be discussing the proposed union of England and Scotland – a project dear to James but to no one else – Salisbury doubted privately whether the absentees would necessarily have been warned – it could represent their silent opposition to the union. It was agreed, anyway, that the Lord Chamberlain should direct a search on 4 November. The real reason for this delay was to ensure that the actual discovery of the plot should take place on Tuesday, 5 November, the king's lucky day and date.

On the afternoon of 4 November the Lord Chamberlain, the Earl of Suffolk, went to the Parliament House, accompanied (at his own request) by the Lord Mounteagle. After visiting the House of Lords they looked at the vaults and cellars on the ground floor.

They remarked the great store of coals and wood there, and perceived Fawkes standing in a corner. The Lord Chamberlain, with affected carelessness, inquired to whom this large provision of fuel belonged; and being informed that the cellar and its contents belonged to Percy, and that he had rented it for about a year and a half, retired without making any more particular search, to report to the King. On their way, Lord Mounteagle expressed his fears and suspicions that some mischief was intended . . .[9]

The king now ordered a thorough search, the task being given to Sir Thomas Knevet, a Westminster magistrate and Gentleman of the Privy Chamber, who set out to do this, properly accompanied, a little before midnight. It could have been done the previous afternoon or on the following morning but there was something more dramatic about the midnight hour and the chosen date. Meanwhile, what of the conspirators? After the Lord Chamberlain's visit Guy Fawkes went to report what had happened. It was agreed that all was well and that Guy should return to his post.

What had happened among the conspirators since Mounteagle's letter had reached the Secretary of State? First of all, Thomas Ward, who had read the letter to Mounteagle, sent a warning to Thomas Winter, his colleague in Mounteagle's service. Winter warned Catesby and they both agreed that the letter must have been written by Tresham, who joined them, however, at White Webbs on 30 October and more or less convinced them of his innocence. Quite apart from oaths he had, in fact, an alibi, having been out of town on the 26th. They would have killed him at once had his protests not carried conviction. It is possible that Catesby had a friend in the Earl of Salisbury's household and that he now made inquiries there as to whether there seemed to be any crisis. He was evidently satisfied that there was none. The letter was clearly thought to be a hoax. So the conspirators held a meeting at Percy's lodging in London on Sunday, 3 November, their last before the opening of Parliament and Catesby's last opportunity to brief his colleagues or those of them who were there: Thomas Percy, the two Wrights and Guy Fawkes. Percy had returned from the north and had rendered his accounts to the Earl of Northumberland, possibly foiled in his plans to abscond with the money. Tresham was not present but Tom Winter saw him that evening in Lincoln's Inn Walks. He appeared to be frantic, convinced that the plot had been discovered, and that they could only save themselves by flight. This was reported to the others who decided nevertheless to wait until the following day. Catesby and John Wright should then set off for Dunchurch, Percy and Thomas Winter remain in London and Guy Fawkes return to his cellar. Christopher Wright, finally, was given the task of watching events at Westminster. Catesby seems to have wavered at this time, despairing at one moment and sure that all was discovered but optimistic at other times and convinced (on the 4th) that all was well. He said as much to Rookwood and Keyes. All the other conspirators were in the midlands and about to make their way to the rendezvous at Dunchurch, where those in London, apart from Fawkes, would eventually join them.

Early on the morning of 5 November, soon after the midnight hour had struck, Sir Thomas Knevet came to the cellar door at the moment Guy Fawkes was leaving. He was promptly put under arrest while the coals and firewood were tossed aside, revealing thirty-six barrels of gunpowder. Fawkes, being searched, was found to have a watch, slow matches and touchwood, together with the lantern he was carrying, which is now in the Bodleian Library at Oxford. When questioned in the king's presence, Guy gave his name as John Johnson, servant to Thomas Percy, and explained that:

... When the King had come to the Parliament House that day, and the Upper House had been sitting, he meant to have fired the match and fled for his own safety before the powder had taken fire; and that if he had not been apprehended that night, he had blown up the Upper House, when the King, Lords, Bishops and others had been there.[10]

Explicit as he was in admitting his intentions, Guy Fawkes would say nothing more and denied having any associates. He was taken downriver by boat to the Tower of London, where Sir William Wade was waiting to receive him. Sir William, it was believed, had ways of persuading people to talk.

6

Fiasco

T the time of Guy Fawkes's arrest the Earl of
Salisbury's information about the conspiracy was incomplete. He knew what Mounteagle had told him
but he rightly concluded that Mounteagle did not,
of necessity, know it all. A number of arrests were
made, a Captain Whitlock being committed to the Tower. 'Sir
Walter Raleigh is much suspected to be a privy to this action' but
here the sleuths were up against the perfect alibi – Raleigh already
being a prisoner in the Tower. On the morning, moreover, of
5 November a number of obvious precautions were taken. The
king's attendance in Parliament was cancelled and guards were
mounted on all the approaches to Westminster and Whitehall. The
Lord Mayor was advised of a state of emergency and told to guard
the city gates, other measures being taken as if to deal with the sort
of disturbance for which the Earl of Essex had once been responsible. To Christopher Wright, who was playing the part of an
innocent bystander, it was manifest that the plot had failed. There
was no massive explosion but, instead, all the signs of a government
now thoroughly alert. The streets were buzzing with rumours but
there was no information to be had. So Christopher Wright left
London at once by the road through Highgate. Keyes followed suit
and so did Rookwood, who had placed relays of horses all the way to
Dunchurch. Last to leave was Thomas Winter, who stayed behind
to collect the latest news. Well mounted as he was, Rookwood suc-
cessively came up with Catesby and John Wright, Percy and
Christopher Wright. They arrived that evening at Catesby's house,

74

Ashby St Leger, having covered eighty miles in the day and Rookwood having ridden 'thirty miles of one horse in two hours'. They need not have hurried because there was no immediate pursuit. Percy was the wanted man and it was assumed that he would be on his way to York. John Lepton was sent after him, who in turn sent a message to the Council of the North and the port authorities at Hull. In Percy's case there was this further confusion about the money he might or might not have purloined. When asked to assist in the hunt for Percy, the Earl of Northumberland was (understandably) more anxious about his money than about Percy's part in the conspiracy. In the event, Percy fled with the other plotters and was with the rest at Ashby St Leger. The only conspirator who remained in London was Tresham, who went about openly until his arrest on the 12th. He had been named by Fawkes on the 10th and might have been arrested on that day. In the meanwhile he was, no doubt, shadowed and the hope may have been that he would lead the secret agents to one of the Jesuits and so incriminate them as being privy to the plot.

The government could have pursued Catesby to his home but the better plan was clearly to allow the gathering to take place at Dunchurch, so identifying all who were concerned in the plot. On 7 November, before Guy Fawkes had been induced to name his confederates, a proclamation was issued calling for the arrest of Catesby, Thomas Winter, Percy, John Wright, Christopher Wright, John Grant, Robert Winter and Ambrose Rookwood. Omitted from the list are Sir Everard Digby, Tresham and Bates; presumably the names unknown to Mounteagle, two of them rather recent recruits and one of them of no importance. Examined by Sir William Wade, Fawkes revealed his proper name on the 7th but would say nothing about his accomplices other than Percy whose name was already known as the tenant of the vault. He was told that their flight had made it possible to identify them, to which he replied that, in that case, his own evidence was superfluous. It was thought on the 7th that he was about to confess everything but Wade reported to Salisbury on the 8th that Fawkes was 'in a most stubborn and perverse humour, as dogged as if he were possessed . . . so sullen and obstinate as there is no dealing with him'. Fawkes then went to the rack and promised, under torture, that he would name his accomplices on the following day, the 10th. He did so, signing his statement with a faint and trembling hand. He had endured the torture so as to gain five days for his friends. They had the chance to escape – not a very good chance, perhaps – but they did not take it. Instead, they went on with the plan as agreed.

On 29 October Sir Everard Digby moved with his family from his own house at Goathurst to Coughton Hall, near Alcester. On Sunday, 3 November, he reached Dunchurch with his followers and servants. Robert Winter left Huddington on the 3rd, spent that night at Grafton with John Talbot, his father-in-law, was joined by the younger Acton of Ribbesford and then met with Humphrey and Stephen Littleton at Coventry. With these and other supporters he reached Dunchurch and, leaving his friends, rode to Ashby St Leger for an expected meeting there with Catesby. That evening Catesby arrived together with Percy, the two Wrights and Rookwood, all exhausted and covered in dirt. Robert Winter now learnt of the disaster and it was decided to join the rest at Dunchurch. There, at the Red Lion, they found Sir Everard Digby playing cards after supper with his uncle Sir Robert Digby of Coleshill, his brother George, a cousin called James, together with Humphrey and Stephen Littleton. 'The six fugitive conspirators, all bespattered with the mire of November high roads, with dejected looks and jaded aspect arrived in due time to tell their tale.' The result was that Sir Robert Digby departed at once and so did Humphrey Littleton and some others. The party remaining numbered about thirty and Catesby proposed that they should make for Wales, trying to collect reinforcements on the way in Warwickshire, Worcestershire and Staffordshire. Their efforts were hopeless from the outset and that for two reasons. First, their party included no one man of sufficient consequence. Their hopes centred on recruiting John Talbot of Grafton, who stood in line to succeed as Earl of Shrewsbury, but he would not have been important enough had he joined – which actually he did not. In the second place, the failure of the Gunpowder Plot made any other efforts hopeless. Instead of being able to say 'The king and Salisbury are dead – now we can capture

London!' they could merely say 'Rebel with us against King James!'
It is surprising that they met with any response at all.

The party left Dunchurch at ten that night and rode to Warwick
where they broke open a stable and 'acquired' some fresh horses,
leaving their own in exchange. Robert Winter objected to this
lawbreaking, to which Catesby replied:

'Some of us may not look back.'

'Others of us, I hope, may,' Winter retorted, 'and therefore I
pray you, let this alone!'

'What, hast thou any hope, Robin? I assure thee, there is none
that knoweth of this action but shall perish!'

Catesby rightly saw himself as a dead man. The pity is that his
followers included men who had known nothing of the plot, who
merely expected a campaign in Flanders, who may indeed have
expected no more than a day's sport. What story had Catesby told
to each of them? Now they were caught up in events they did not
understand, some being servants who had done no more than they
were told. They were all guilty by their association with the conspirators and became more guilty with each hour that passed. From
Warwick the party went on to Grant's house at Norbrook, where
they collected some arms and armour, and so to Winter's house at
Huddington where they slept the night. On the Thursday morning
they went to Whewell Grange, Lord Windsor's house, and helped
themselves to more arms. From there they rode on, about sixty in
number, to Holbeach, Stephen Littleton's house near Stourbridge in
Staffordshire, where Sir Everard Digby, Humphrey Littleton,
Robert Winter and various other members of the party deserted.
Those remaining knew now that they had come to the end of the
road. They had become aware during the night that the house was
being watched. It is difficult to understand what the conspirators
were now hoping to achieve. Had they not wasted time trying to
increase their numbers the leaders might have reached the coast and
might have had a chance to escape by sea. By going from house to
house, collecting followers and weapons, they had made escape
impossible. Holbeach was capable of defence but what good would
they do by defending it? They could fight to the end but these were

religious men whose beliefs had drawn them into this ill-fated enterprise. How could they, in conscience, fire upon the Sheriff's men, inflicting casualties among men of the posse comitatus, men summoned from the fields to help enforce the law? And what good would it do? They would be killed or taken in the end. It seems, nevertheless, that they made preparations for battle. Thomas Winter went out to reconnoitre and Catesby, Grant and Rookwood set about idiotically drying their stock of gunpowder on a platter before the kitchen fire. It was inevitably touched off by an ember and blew up in their faces, leaving them injured, shaken and terrified. When Winter, returning, asked what he meant to do, Catesby said, 'We mean here to die,' to which Winter replied, 'I will take such part as you do.'

So far there had only been scouts sent to keep in touch. On Friday morning, at about eleven, the forces of Sir Richard Verney, Sheriff of Warwickshire, were joined at Holbeach by the forces of Sir Richard Walsh, Sheriff of Worcestershire. As these levies closed in on the house a few shots were fired, which made them pause. Walsh brought forward and posted two good marksmen, Thomas Hall and John Street. Presently the leaders of the rebel force came out of the house and into the courtyard. Thomas Winter received a bolt from a crossbow in his right shoulder, putting his arm out of action. John Wright was shot dead at the same time and Christopher Wright mortally wounded. Ambrose Rookwood was badly wounded and John Grant disabled. Catesby called to Thomas Percy: 'Stand by me, Tom, and we will die together.' They stood back to back, sword in hand, and John Street killed them both 'with two bullets at one shott out of his musket'. The others surrendered as the Sheriffs' men rushed into the courtyard. Not all the conspirators were there, however, and others were hunted down over the next few days. Keyes was arrested in Warwickshire, probably on his way to join the others. Sir Everard Digby was arrested after a long pursuit. Those who were at large for the longest time were Robert Winter and Stephen Littleton, who lay hidden for weeks at a time and were not betrayed until after two months on the run. These were taken in the end and so were many possible accomplices and witnesses, all of whom were examined at length. Among those questioned was Marmaduke Ward, who was quickly released again despite the suspicious nature of his movements. The skirmish at Holbeach was in itself a trifling affair, with little resistance from the rebels and no acts of heroism to be recorded on the side of law and order. The man singled out for commendation was John Street, the marksman, who was awarded a pension of two shillings a day for his 'extraordinary service' in killing the two leaders. If we multiply by forty, say, to find the modern equivalent, his pension could now be worth about £1,500 a year; a generous reward for that single shot. It is to be assumed that his task, defined by Walsh on Salisbury's instructions, was to prevent Percy being taken alive. It would have been awkward to have a prisoner claiming in his defence that he had tried to betray his friends but that nobody in Salisbury's household would listen. To have killed Catesby as well was perhaps less meritorious but it is arguable that he too may have known too much.

The man who more or less escaped the vengeance of the law was Francis Tresham. He was not arrested and brought before the Council until 12 November when he tried to show that he had not been in the plot. On the following day he submitted a written statement in which he admitted to a knowledge of the plot since 15 October but claimed to have done his best to discourage it.

Thus neither my hand, purse or head was either in the acting or contriving of this plot; but being lately and unexpectedly fallen into it, I sought, by all the argument I could, to dissuade it: the silence I used was only to deliver myself from that infamous brand of an accuser, and to save Catesby's life, which is all true rules I was bound to do.[1]

It was true, of course, that Tresham had not been active in the plot. The trouble was that he knew of it and did nothing to warn the authorities; so that he was, on his own admission, guilty of misprision of treason. He was committed to the Tower but not examined again immediately, the members of the Council now having the other conspirators to examine. They were chiefly anxious to implicate the Jesuits who had been privy, by Winter's account, to the mission to Spain under Elizabeth (see page 45). On the 13th they

79

extracted from Tresham his admission that Garnet knew about this
mission.

Soon after his imprisonment this miserable man was attacked by a dangerous
and painful disease, which had reduced him to the extremity of weakness, and
rendered it necessary that his wife and a confidential servant should constantly
attend him. On the 15th December, the Lieutenant of the Tower writes to
Lord Salisbury, 'Tresham is worse and worse. To-morrow I have appointed
a consultation for him of three doctors. If he escape, it must be by great care
and good providence that he may die of that kind of death he most deserveth.'[2]

A few days later Tresham dictated to his servant, Vavasour, a
letter in which he retracted his statement about Father Garnet and
added, for good measure, that he had not seen Garnet for sixteen
years. The letter was then signed by him, witnessed by Vavasour and
another servant and entrusted to Mrs Tresham for delivery to the
Earl of Salisbury. Tresham died in the Tower on 23 December
'with very great pain'. Wrote Wade on this occasion, 'I find his
friends were marvellous confident if had escaped this sickness and
have given out words in this place that they feared not the course of
justice.' Soon after Tresham's death his body was examined by
'Butler, the great physician of Cambridge', who gave it as his
opinion that Tresham had been poisoned.

Tresham's career has given rise to two interesting theories,
neither to be ignored. It has been stated with great confidence that
it was Tresham who wrote the letter to Mounteagle and that it was
he, in effect, who betrayed the plot. This was certainly the conclusion reached by the other conspirators and two of them, as we have
seen, came near to killing him. We must doubt, however, whether
this theory is tenable. Apart from his alibi and apart from his success
in convincing Catesby and Winter, the essential fact remains that he
made no claim to have written the letter. His position, we must
remember, was that of heir apparent to a big estate, an heir whose
father did not die until 1605. He came into money at the very time
of the plot and could afterwards have assumed a very respectable
position in society. He was happily married and looked to the future
of his children. Charged or about to be charged with treason, with

death very near, he would wish above all things to provide for his widow and his descendants. Had he written the letter this was the moment to say so. 'Treason?' he should have said. 'It was I who *frustrated* the plot!' But there was no word from him about that. It is true that his friends 'feared not the course of justice' but they could argue, after all, that he had done nothing to further the conspiracy, neither digging in the mine nor joining in the midland rising. On his deathbed he was capable of dictating a letter but instead of exonerating himself his effort went into withdrawing his earlier statement about Garnet, who was not even in custody. As the evidence he had given did nothing to incriminate Garnet in the Gunpowder Plot and as his retraction was made nonsense by his obviously false claim not to have seen Garnet for sixteen years, his last letter did no good to anybody. Neither did it do anything to save his estate for his family. All he could do for the Treshams – being unable to claim the authorship of the letter – was to take poison and so die before he could be tried. He would thus be dead before he could be condemned and dead indeed before he was even indicted. This, he might suppose, would save his estate from confiscation as part of a sentence for treason. He was not entirely right about this but he had studied law and could reasonably have concluded that this was the legal position. One should not be dogmatic about the poison on such slight evidence as the one medical opinion but he had the motive, and the access to him of his confidential servant might have given him the means. It would be reasonable to guess that his illness had been real but not fatal in itself and that poison finished what nature had begun.

The other theory, that put forward by Father Francis Edwards, is that Catesby, Percy, Fawkes and Tresham were all spies in government pay, that Salisbury had initiated the plot and assigned the role of each conspirator, and that Tresham – having played his part – was allowed to escape from the Tower and spend the rest of his life abroad. This is an attractive theory but it leaves one to wonder why Tresham should have been spared while the others were sacrificed. That Salisbury was capable of killing off agents who had served their purpose is possibly true. But was he the man to discard the majority and save the one exception? If we are to suppose, moreover, that Tresham was a government agent, how do we account for Salisburys treatment of Mounteagle? His reward was a pension of £700 a year, the equivalent of, say, £28,000 in today's debased currency, the sort of salary we might allocate to the chairman of a nationalized industry. Could he have deserved that for revealing a conspiracy which Salisbury himself was directing? And supposing he did deserve it why should Tresham, another agent, deserve no more than exile in a minor diplomatic post? It would have been simpler to give Tresham some of the credit and half of the pension. To arrange his escape from the Tower was perfectly feasible but was it necessary? There is much, perhaps, we shall never know about the Gunpowder Plot but the theories of Father Edwards would seem to create as many problems as they purport to solve. It is simply not credible that Guy Fawkes should have died expecting a last-minute reprieve for how could anyone escape the gallows whose attempted crime had been to destroy the king in Parliament? If that were not beyond forgiveness, what crime could be more serious? If Guy Fawkes were to live, who on earth could deserve to hang?

From the Earl of Salisbury's point of view, the plot was, so far, an almost complete success. All that it lacked was evidence to incriminate the Jesuits. Towards finding such evidence a useful step would be to secure some of the Jesuits themselves and notably those associated with the conspirators now awaiting trial. One of these would be Father Garnet, Superior of the Order in England, and the others might be Father Tesimond and Father Gerard. All were known to be active in the south midlands and all were certainly well known to the conspirators. It may seem proper to ask, at the outset, whether they had been involved. The answer must be that they were not. It is clear, moreover, that they were opposed to any such plot as being at once unlawful and impolitic. The policy of the pope, as known to Father Parsons and Father Garnet, was to reach some agreement with King James. A Catholic plot against him was therefore the last thing they would want to encourage. As against that, they had been in close contact with the conspirators at the time of the plot. When Sir Everard Digmy moved from Goathurst to

Coughton Hall, Father Garnet was with him. When the plot failed Digby wrote to Garnet from Norbrook, explaining what had happened, and the letter was carried to Coughton by Catesby's servant, Bates. In his reply, Garnet 'marvelled that they would enter into such wicked actions and not be ruled by the advice of friends and the order of his Holiness given to all'. But Garnet had not been wholly ignorant of it. There had been meetings at White Webbs and elsewhere and it is scarcely credible that Garnet should have failed to notice the unusual activity. When Thomas Bates came to be examined on 13 January 1606, he described how Garnet received the message, going on to state,

... that Garnet and Greenway conferred together for about half an hour, while he walked in the hall; after which Greenway came out and accompanied him to Huddington, where he talked for some time privately with Catesby, and then rode away to Mr. Abington's in Worcestershire, for the purpose of persuading that gentleman to join the insurgents.[3]

Limited as this admission might be, it was thought to be enough. Two days later a proclamation went forth for the arrest as traitors of the three Jesuits who had been accessory to the plot and threatening dire penalties against all who should harbour, maintain or conceal them or should not do his best to bring about their discovery and apprehension. Gerard and Greenway escaped and left the country but Garnet, accompanied by Nicholas Owen (a lay brother), went to Hinlip, a house well provided with places in which to hide, where Father Oldcorne was already in residence. Unfortunately for Garnet the likelihood of his being there was betrayed by Humphrey Littleton 'being in danger of his life' and hearing 'large promises of favour and rewards'. The result was that the Sheriff of Worcestershire, Sir Henry Bromley, came to Hinlip on 20 January 'with a seemly troop of his own attendants', and presented Mr Thomas Habington with a search warrant.

Bromley knew the house well; he had searched it before. First he examined the long gallery over the gatehouse. There he found two of the dozen or more hiding places ... so ingeniously framed and with such art as it cost much labour ere they could be found.

As the search proceeded there other secret places were found, 'contrived with no less skill and industry . . .'[4]

The search continued for a week but failed, the hidden priests being finally starved into surrender. They came out on 27 January, Oldcorne being immediately identified and Garnet recognized at Holt Castle where Bromley lived. By the time Garnet was brought to trial all the conspirators had been tried and executed. When we come to study Garnet's trial we shall do well to remember what the Earl of Salisbury had to say about it. His object, he made it clear, was not to convict and punish Garnet but to make a 'public and visible anatomy of Popish doctrine and practice'. As for the previous trial of the conspirators themselves, the Attorney-General Sir Edward Coke was briefed beforehand by the Secretary of State. Coke was to make it appear to the world that the conspiracy began before Queen Elizabeth died. It was urged that the plot was the result of the king's policy towards the Catholics but the conspiracy began 'before his Majesty's face was ever seen, or that he had done anything in government'.

Next, you must, in any case, when you speak of the letter which was the first ground of discovery, absolutely disclaim that any of these (the accused) wrote it, though you leave the further judgement indefinite who else it should be. Lastly, and that you must omit, you must not deliver, in commendation of my Lord Mounteagle, words to show how sincerely he dealt, and how fortunately it proved that he was the instrument of so great a blessing as this was . . . because it is so loudly given out that he was once of this plot of powder, and afterwards betrayed it all to me . . .[5]

To this was added a postscript. 'You must remember to lay Owen as foul in this as you can.'

Here, then, is a clear, if not complete, statement of public policy. The conspiracy must be shown to have begun before James came to the throne. So it had, in a way. There must be no official conclusion about the authorship of the letter and there must be plenty of praise for Lord Mounteagle. Nothing must be said to support the rumour that Mounteagle had been one of the conspirators and had betrayed the rest. But why was it so important to deny that story – unless it were nearly the truth? It is true that Mounteagle had never been a sworn member of the gang but he was near enough to them to know what they were plotting. The inconvenience of that rumour was that it detracted from the king's wisdom in discovering what the letter meant. As for the authorship of the letter, that should remain a mystery for the same reason, helping the king see the discovery of the plot as essentially his own doing. That none of the accused had written the letter is clear enough for none of them claimed to have written it. Coke would be on safe ground, therefore, in excluding them. As for Owen, the intelligence expert serving with Sir William Stanley in Flanders, it would certainly serve the government's purpose to suggest that the conspiracy extended to Sir William's camp. It could be no more than a suggestion, however, and proof of it was notably absent. That Sir William knew about the plot is more than probable, Guy Fawkes having been sent to tell him about it; but he was not otherwise involved and there was no call for action on his part. The conspiracy seems to have begun and ended with the men who had died and the men who were in the dock.

— 7 —

Westminster Hall

The trials of Robert Winter, Thomas Winter, Guy Fawkes, John Grant, Ambrose Rookwood, Robert Keyes, and Thomas Bates, at Westminster, by a Special Commission for High Treason, being Conspirators in the Gunpowder Plot, 3 Jac. I, 27 January 1606.
The Commissioners were:

Charles, Earl of Nottingham, Lord High Admiral of England.
Thomas, Earl of Suffolk, Steward of the Household.
Edward, Earl of Worcester, Master of the Horse.
Charles, Earl of Devonshire, Master of the Ordnance.
Henry, Earl of Northampton, Warden of the Cinque Ports.
Robert, Earl of Salisbury, Principal Secretary of State.
The Lord Chief Justice of England, Sir John Popham.
The Lord Chief Baron of the Exchequer, Sir Thomas Fleming.
Sir Thomas Walmisley and Sir Peter Warburton, Kts, both of
    them Justices of the Common Pleas.

These Commissioners formed no ordinary court and this was no ordinary occasion. All the examinations, whether of the accused or of witnesses, had taken place previously. All the statements had been taken, all the evidence had been sifted at these earlier examinations. At the actual trial the Attorney-General would provide a summary of the evidence and would ask the jury for a verdict. The verdict was a foregone conclusion and the object of the trial was merely to publicize the case for the prosecution. The indictment was itself no ordinary document because it named various persons who were not

there. Those named as false traitors were in this order, Henry
Garnet, Oswald Tesimond (or Greenway), John Gerard, all of them
Jesuits; Robert Winter, Esquire; Thomas Winter, gentleman;
Guido Fawkes, gentleman; John Grant, Esquire; Robert Keyes,
gentleman; Ambrose Rookwood, Esquire and Thomas Bates,
Yeoman. Also included in the indictment were Robert Catesby and
Thomas Percy, Esquires, John and Christopher Wright, gentlemen
(in open rebellion, lately slain) and Francis Tresham, Esquire (lately
dead). So the men on trial comprised three priests, one of them not
yet known to be in custody, and two of them actually overseas, seven
prisoners in court and five men already dead. The trial of those
deceased was not an empty form because the property would be
forfeit of those convicted of treason. The trial of the absent was also
useful in emphasizing their supposed part in the plot. Yet another
odd circumstance (at least to the modern mind) is that the case for
the prosecution had already been published in a work of which the
king was supposed to be the author. But the oddest aspect of the
trial was that the judges and the public present comprised the intended victims of the crime. In the great Hall of Westminster 'the
Queen and Prince were in a secret place by to hear and some say the
King in another' and most of the seats were reserved for members of
the Lords and Commons, the very people who would have perished
had the plot succeeded. So the Attorney-General could fairly claim
that the crime intended was 'such as no man can express it – no
example pattern it – no measure contain it'. This did not mean,
however, that words failed him, for he spoke, in fact, for hours.

Sir Edward Coke's speech has been described as tedious, which it
may well have been, but it fairly summarized the government's
message to the public at large and to Christendom as a whole. As
urged by Salisbury, the Attorney-General went back to the treasonable correspondence with Spain in Elizabeth's time, matters not
included in the indictment, but he came more to the point in his
denunciation of the Jesuits:

By these Jesuits was Catesby resolved that this fact of the Powder Treason
was both lawful and meritorious, and herewith be persuaded and settled the

rest when they seemed to hesitate. So that the principal offenders are the seducing Jesuits; men that use the reverence of religion Yea, even the most sacred and blessed name of Jesus as a mantle to cover their impiety, and treason. And surely the Jesuits were so far engaged in this treason, so that some of them did not stick to say, when they heard it had miscarried that they were utterly undone.[1]

He went on to dwell upon the romish doctrine that a king might be deposed by the Church. This allowed him to digress a little for the benefit of an unseen member of his audience, remarking of his Sovereign that:

... if he were not a king by descent, yet deserved he to be made one for his rare and excellent endowments and ornaments both of body and mind. Look into his true and constant religion and piety, his justice, his learning above all kings christened, his acumen, his judgment, his memory ...[2]

Having made that point, Sir Edward emphasized that the crime was planned in the very first year of his reign and that 'they had treason on foot against that King before they saw his face in England'. He traced this iniquity to the Bull of Excommunication against Queen Elizabeth, who had nevertheless been remarkably lenient towards the papists. The Attorney-General tried to describe the intended crime: 'Lord! what a wind, what a fire, what a commotion of earth and air there would have been!' but he was rather more successful in dealing with 'the admirable discovery of this treason, which was by one of themselves, who had taken the oath and sacrament, as hath been said, against his own will'. This allowed him to wonder:

How the King was divinely illuminated by almighty God, 'the only ruler of princes,' like an angel of God, to direct and point, as it were, to the very place, to cause a search to be made there, out of those dark words of the letter concerning 'a terrible blow'.[3]

There followed a reading of some of the evidence, being the signed confessions of the accused and other documents in the case. After that the Lord Chief Justice addressed the Jury and then directed them to retire and consider their verdict.

The trial followed of Sir Everard Digby. His was a separate case because he was arraigned under an indictment taken at Wellingborough before a Northampton Grand Jury and so delivered to the Special Commission sitting at Westminster. Sir Everard pleaded guilty to the charge of treason but pleaded for the interests of his wife and son (whose property was entailed), his sisters and creditors, asking for himself that he should be beheaded rather than suffer a traitor's death. To this there was a response from the Attorney-General 'but in respect of the time (for it grew now dark), very briefly'. On the subject of Sir Everard's estate Sir Edward exclaimed:

. . . Oh, how he doth now put on the bowels of nature and compassion in the peril of his private and domestical estate! But before, when the public state of his country, when the King, the Queen, the tender princes, the nobles, the whole kingdom were designed to a perpetual destruction; where was then this piety, this religious affection, this care?

. . . And for his wife and children, whereas he said, that for the Catholic cause he was content to neglect the ruin of himself, his wife, his estate and all; he should have his desire as it is in the Psalm, 'Let his wife be a widow, and his children vagabonds; let his posterity be destroyed, and in the next generation let his name be quite put out.' He concluded that these things must be left to the pleasure of his Majesty and the course of justice and law.[4]

The proceedings might reasonably have concluded soon after this but now the Earl of Northamptonshire made a long speech addressed to Sir Everard Digby. The point of this was that Northampton was supposed to be a Catholic, his intervention marking the distinction between loyal Catholics and Jesuited traitors. Speaking for the government, he set out to destroy the story that the king had, before his accession, promised the Catholics a new measure of toleration which was afterwards denied them.

But touching the truth of the matters it will be witnessed by many, that this traitor Percy, after both the first and second return from the King, brought to the Catholics no spark of comfort, of encouragement, of hope; whereof no stronger proof of argument doth need, than that Fawkes and others were employed both into Spain, and other parts . . . after Percy's coming back; as

89

in likelihood, they should not have been, in case he had returned with a branch of olive in his mouth . . .[5]

If we are to believe the printed account we must suppose that Northampton spoke at intolerable length and latterly perhaps in darkness. It is probable, however, that the printed version was expanded so as to include all he might have said, with classical allusions and reference to holy writ, complete also with that telling comparison with the Siege of Troy in which the horse's belly was stuffed, 'not as in old time with armed Greeks, but with Hellish gunpowder'.

It was left to the Earl of Salisbury to sum up the case for the Crown and he did so briefly, emphasizing, as Northampton had done, that the King had never at any time 'given the least hope, much less promise of toleration'. He referred to the fact that Digby had at first denied having any part in the Gunpowder Plot and showed from Fawkes's testimony that this plea was nonsense.

Next the said Earl did justly and greatly commend the Lord Mounteagle for his loyal and honourable care of his Prince and country, in the speedy bringing forth of the letter sent unto him; wherein, he said, that he had showed both his discretion and fidelity . . .[6]

Upon the conclusion of the speech of the Earl of Salisbury, Sergeant Philips prayed the judgment of the Court upon the verdict of the Jury against the first seven prisoners, and against Sir Everard Digby upon his own confession. The prisoners were then asked whether they had anything to say against judgment of death being pronounced against them. Digby spoke but his speech was not reported. Rookwood pleaded, as an extenuating circumstance, that 'he had been neither author nor actor, but only persuaded and drawn in by Catesby, whom he loved above any worldly man'. Keyes said, 'that his estate and fortunes were desperate, and as good now as another time and for this cause rather than another'. The others had little to say except to crave for mercy. After that the Lord Chief Justice pronounced judgment of high treason upon all the prisoners. The trial was over and the prisoners were taken back to the Tower.

On the following Thursday, 30 January, Sir Everard Digby,

Robert Winter, John Grant and Thomas Bates were drawn upon hurdles to a scaffold erected at the western end of St Paul's Church-yard. Everything had been done to make the spectacle as imposing as possible. None of the condemned men had anything much to say on the scaffold and it is possible that their attitude as martyrs for the faith had been somewhat spoilt by lack of support from their own Church.

George Blackwell, the Archpriest, has sent out a letter to all Catholics protesting that this plot is against the prescript of a general Council . . . private violent attempts cannot be thought of, much less aided and maintained by Catholics. For his own part, if any notice had been given him, he would have been most forward by all possible means to have stayed and suppressed the attempt.[7]

In a letter to his wife, written from the Tower, Sir Everard commented upon this ecclesiastical disapproval and added:

If I had thought there had been the least sin in it, I would not have been of it for all the world, and no other cause drew me to hazard my fortune and life but zeal to God's religion. But when I heard that Catholics and priests thought that it should be a great sin that should be the cause of my end, it called my conscience in doubt of my very best actions and intentions. I protest unto you that the doubts I had of my own good state, which only proceeded from the censure of others, caused more bitterness of grief in me than all the miseries that ever I endured; and I could do nothing but with tears ask pardon at God's hands for all my errors, both in actions and intentions in this business.[8]

Digby thus acknowledged that the whole plot was morally wrong. John Grant thought otherwise and said, on the day of his execution, 'I am satisfied that our project was so far from being sinful, that I rely entirely upon my merits in bearing a part of that noble action . . . [as expiation for all previous sins].

All these four were executed, being hanged, drawn and quartered. On the following day, Friday, Thomas Winter, Ambrose Rook-wood, Robert Keyes and Guido Fawkes were drawn on hurdles to a scaffold set up near the scene of the intended crime. The only significant speech came from Rookwood, who prayed God to make the king a Catholic. Guy Fawkes suffered last, being almost too weak from torture to climb the ladder but finally jumped and broke his neck with the fall. So far as the conspiracy itself is concerned that is practically the end of the story. But the Earl of Salisbury wanted to use the plot for other purposes. He had conveyed his message to the Catholics, to the people at large and to the other kingdoms in Europe. But there was more to do before all was done.

On 6 November, the rumours began to circulate about the Earl of Northumberland:

This Thomas Percy hath been a servant of the Earl of Northumberland and was put in great trust by him concerning his northern business and is lately made by him a Pensioner. Early on Sunday morning the Earl of Worcester was sent to Essex House to signify the matter to the Earl of Northumberland, whom he found asleep in his bed, and who hath done since his best endeavour for his apprehension. This Percy, my Lord of Northumberland confesseth, had £4,000 of his in his hands . . .

7th November. The Earl of Northumberland is committed to the charge of the Archbishop.

11th November. The Earl of Northumberland, who is now under restraint at the house of the Archbishop in Croydon, being in question for some matter concerning Thomas Percy, his Steward, protesteth that though Percy saw him at Sion House upon the Monday before the plot yet it was but by chance, and that Percy had cheated him of his Northern rents by some lying tale, five horse-loads of money, £3,000 and more.[9]

With the Earl of Northumberland under open arrest, the conduct of some other peers was brought in question. On the day for which the explosion had been planned certain of the Catholic peers were absent from Parliament. Why? Had they been warned and yet said nothing about it? Inquiries continued for months and it was 3 June before Lords Stourton and Mordaunt were brought before the Star Chamber. Stourton made a confused plea about having no money, being in debt, his wife just delivered, her father just died. Failing to come on Tuesday, he *had* been present on Friday. Mordaunt had no real excuse and had been seen talking with Catesby. The result was that Mordaunt was fined 10,000 marks, Stourton 6,000, and both to remain in the Tower during his Majesty's pleasure. Mordaunt might have been warned by Robert Keyes, a member of his household.

His fine was remitted after his death in 1608. Lord Montague was also brought before the Star Chamber and was lucky, perhaps, to escape with a fine of £4,000 – he might have been warned by Guy Fawkes, once his servant. All these, however, were small fry. The real drama began when the Earl of Northumberland was brought to the Tower on 23 June, together with his brother, Sir Allan Percy. There was real difficulty about framing the indictment against the earl but the Attorney-General had done his best. He finally listed six charges, as follows:

(1) For endeavouring to be the head of the English Papists and to procure them toleration.

(2) For admitting and placing Thomas Percy to be one of the King's Gentlemen Pensioners without ministering unto him the Oath of Supremacy, knowing Percy to be a recusant.

(3) That when he was commanded to keep his house upon discovery of the treason he wrote two letters to his friends in the North parts (supposing Percy to have fled thither) to have a care of his money and revenues, but utterly neglecting in those letters to take any order for the apprehension of Percy.

(4) For presuming to write letters abroad after his restraint without leave of the King or the Council.

(5) That being a Privy Councillor he had more care of his treasure than that of the King and the State.

(6) That his letters to the North part were to give a watchword to Percy to further his escape, and besides that he had confessed that since his Majesty's reign he had conference concerning the King's nobility and how long, and in what manner, he would reign.[10]

In summarizing the case against Northumberland, Sir Edward Coke is said to have argued that:

In the beginning to the King's reign and at the end of the Queen's, the Earl of Northumberland became the head of the Catholic cause, and he desired Catholics might depend on him. After the Pope had set forth two damnable bulls against the King, the Earl knowing of them, sent this Percy to Scotland to ask for a toleration of the Catholics, with two letters and a message pretending the more easy entrance if he would give hopes of toleration, which were intolerable and not to be endured, for that an Englishman's heart grieves to see another kind of worship. Upon Percy's return out of Scotland the Earl of Northumberland told the Catholics that the King's commandment was that they should be eased of their persecution, which the King himself *in verbo regis* says he never did promise or command. After this Percy and Catesby plotted their treason and yet soon after Percy was made a Pensioner; a fit man to put an axe into his hands to carry it over the King's head! And not only was he made a pensioner, he never took any oath. Then Master Attorney enlarged upon the other matters of the charges at length and after his accustomed manner . . .[11]

Of this style of advocacy we have had, perhaps, enough, but we may conclude that these proceedings were grossly unfair. Upon all or most of the six counts the Earl may have been persuaded to plead guilty. He was probably unable to deny the truth of (1) and (2). (3) would admit of an explanation – as for example an awareness that other measures had been taken for Percy's arrest – and (5) is virtually the same charge again. The first part of (6) was presumably nonsense and the second part related to the Earl's known interest in astrology. What was the sum total of his evil-doing? That he had trusted Percy and that he had neglected to administer an oath? But the real inequity lay in the fact that the more serious charge was unspoken. Behind all this verbiage 'after his accustomed manner', the Attorney-General was really suggesting that Northumberland, through Thomas Percy, knew all about the plot and probably approved it. Percy was his relative and servant and would not have joined such a conspiracy without informing his employer. Percy had dined at Sion House on 4 November and Fawkes had come to look for Percy there. All this was true and yet proved nothing. Neither, moreover, did Coke try to prove that Northumberland was in the plot. He suggested this by implication and went on to number his six charges, all but one of them trivial but all supported by some sort of evidence. On this basis the Earl was condemned to pay a fine of £30,000, to forfeit all offices under the Crown and to be imprisoned in the Tower for life. He had actually paid £11,000 by 1614, when the rest was remitted, and he remained in the Tower until 1621. In modern currency £30,000 would have been the equivalent of £1,200,000 and even £11,000 would be £440,000. So one more of Salisbury's enemies was put out of mischief for a long time to come. While in the Tower he devoted himself, as the 'Wizard Earl', to astrology and to scientific pursuits and it is pleasing to learn that many men of learning went to visit him.

For the little that could be proved against the Earl of Northumberland his sentence was one of appalling severity. We may fairly ask at this point whether any other sentence could be thought unjust or whether there might not have been a reprieve for any of those whose trial we have described. In commenting on this we must realize, first of all, that the legal position was clear. They were involved in treason, for which the penalty was death. The evidence against them was conclusive and they could not and did not deny that they had earned the death penalty. It is clear, nevertheless, that some were more guilty than others. We cannot have much sympathy for the original five: Catesby, Percy, Thomas Winter, John Wright and Guy Fawkes. Catesby was a plausible, lying, shifty character with powers of leadership and a gift for gaining the loyal devotion of better men. Percy was an older man, completely unreliable and probably more ambitious than devout. Thomas Winter was the best of them and probably the ablest, his religious motives being predominant over any others. It is difficult to see John Wright as anything but an overgrown adolescent, led into mischief by Catesby. As for Guy Fawkes, the unsuccessful soldier, he would seem to have been a religious fanatic and a man of almost inhuman courage. He, one would guess, was destined, by nature, to be the victim or the odd man out; the one at the end of the line, to whom the dangerous or dirty task would be left. Of these five only two were tried and neither could complain of their treatment. There would be no merit in martyrdom if intending martyrs were all reprieved. By their own theology they were right to do what they did. By their own law their oppressors were right to hang them. The essential conflict is there and the eventual execution is unavoidable. Where lunacy creeps in nowadays is in the strike or demonstration against the death penalty being enforced. Martyrdom may serve a purpose in the world but only when the martyr dies. The reprieve makes nonsense of the motives on either side.

Of those who came later to the Gunpowder Plot, Keyes, Bates and Christopher Wright, only two were tried. Robert Keyes was a desperate man, ruined and indebted, who almost welcomed death when it came. For Thomas Bates one has more sympathy. He was merely a servant and his crime was simply to have done as he was told. The incrimination of Garnet, as we shall see, was due to him. He was a devout Catholic, no doubt, but may otherwise have understood only a part of what was happening, whether in the vault or at his trial. He was only sworn in the first place because he had come to know of the plot by accident.

When we come to consider the squires who were to lead the midland revolt – John Grant, Robert Winter, Ambrose Rookwood, Francis Tresham and Sir Everard Digby – we wonder from the outset what Catesby had actually told them. His earlier talk would have been about a regiment of cavalry for service in Flanders; an enterprise which was in no way illegal. Some were thus quite innocently involved in the collection of horses and arms. Later came mention of a plot to restore Catholicism in England, details of which they were sworn to keep secret. But Catesby, in demanding their oath of secrecy, was not under oath to tell them the whole story. There was no need for them to know about the Gunpowder Plot, nor may some of them have known about it until they heard of its failure. These men had been chosen for their wealth, not for their qualities of intellect. John Grant was taciturn and possibly stupid. Robert Winter was merely Thomas's elder brother and much under Thomas's influence. Ambrose Rookwood was well liked but almost solely interested in horses. Francis Tresham was the last of the conspirators to join the plot, a rather wavering and indecisive character who was never brought to trial but was posthumously beheaded as a traitor. Some of these may have suffered more for their stupidity than for their evil intent – as did others, no doubt, like Stephen Littleton, who had not been in the conspiracy at all. There was nothing unjust about their sentences but we may regard them as relatively innocent, guiltless perhaps of intended murder. Of the midland squires the most attractive was Sir Everard Digby, whose crime arose from his being so young and impressionable. With a little luck he might have had a much happier fate. All that remains of Digby is a poem he wrote during his last days beginning 'Who's that which knocks? O, stay, my Lord, I come' together with a few letters and his name carved in the stonework of his cell in Broad Arrow Tower. Tragic as his own life was, however, his son became the famous Sir Kenelm Digby, author, naval commander and diplomatist. Kenelm Digby was only three years old when his father was executed, and he inherited, by his own account, only 'the scant relics' of a shipwrecked estate. These comprised, however, his mother's property and two other manors which had been entailed, so that the Crown was defeated in the effort to take possession of them. Half of Sir Everard's other fortune was given by the king to Sir William Anstruther, one of his Scots followers. There are few men of the seventeenth century who were as distinguished as Sir Kenelm in so many different ways. He was with Prince Charles and the Duke of Buckingham at Madrid in 1623. He defeated a French and Venetian fleet in Scanderoon harbour. He fought a duel in defence of Charles I. The author of several books, one of them on religion, he became a friend of Descartes and did some diplomatic work for Oliver Cromwell. He held office at court after the Restoration and was a founder member of the Royal Society. His final achievement was in discovering the necessity of oxygen to the life of plants. If there was anywhere a happy ending to the Gunpowder Plot it would be found in the astonishing life of Sir Everard Digby's son.

8

The Tower of London

FTER the conspirators had been tried and executed; after the Earl of Northumberland had gone to the Tower, one thing remained to do. It had to be shown that the Jesuits were implicated in the plot. The effort to prove this ended as a duel between two extremely clever men, the Earl of Salisbury and Father Henry Garnet, S J; the sort of duel that has been fought so often in our own time. We have to realize, first of all, that it was never a matter of life or death. From the time of his capture it was clear that the Jesuit was going to be executed – clear to the Council and clear to him. What was not clear was his association with the plot. Death he deserved in any case for becoming a Jesuit and for being in England. Was he also guilty of treason in this particular context? When the court sat at Westminster to try the conspirators, Henry Garnet and two other Jesuits were among the accused, the indictment was one of high treason and the verdict, against all the accused (whether alive or dead, whether there or not), was one of guilty. Technically, that would have justified Garnet's immediate execution as a convicted criminal. Intellectually, that would not do. The Westminster trial began on 27 January 1606, which was actually the day of Garnet's arrest. The plotters were executed on 30 and 31 January but Garnet did not reach the Gatehouse Prison until 11 February nor the Tower until the 14th. It could have been arranged otherwise but the witnesses, who all denied his knowledge of the plot, were all dead before his ordeal began. Some authors have suggested that the government, during this period, could use torture to obtain any evidence to prove anything. This may have been theoretically possible but it was not, in general, what the Earl of Salisbury wanted. If the truth were not quite good enough, the alternative evidence had to look reasonably probable. There must be a convincing story for the people at large, for the courts of Europe and even for posterity. That the Jesuits had caused the plot must be an accepted fact of history for the next hundred years.

In studying this verdict we have to realize, from the outset, that it had a basis of truth. There were Catholics who clung to their faith but were content to lie low, attending mass in private but making no effort to convert anyone else. There were one or two of these on the Privy Council itself. There were, on the other hand, the activists, those who planned to make England Catholic again. The majority of these were unquestionably under Jesuit influence. But for these the papist body would have quietly dwindled and would in time have been absorbed. What was perfectly clear was that all the conspirators had been under Jesuit influence. This was undeniable and was never denied; and the general effect of that influence was to encourage Catholic resistance to governmental pressure. The pupils of the Jesuits were all known recusants, holding meetings, hiding priests, sending their children overseas for schooling, publicly going on pilgrimage and making no secret of their views. To that extent the Jesuits could be held responsible for any plot, any rising, which might occur. But was their responsibility more immediate than that? Was it they who thought of the plot in the first place? Was it they who chose the men who should carry it out? Was the plan drawn up with their advice? From the government's point of view, this would be the ideal conclusion to reach. Failing that (and a failure here was to be expected) the next best thing would be to prove that the Jesuits were, if not the authors of the plot, at least aware of it and did nothing to prevent it. That would be treasonable in itself and would be enough to link the Jesuits with the crime. All sorts of denials would follow but to make this a Jesuit plot, known as such in Spain and France, would be a diplomatic success. To obtain the necessary evidence was not going to be easy, however. Garnet, who had dodged the government agents for twenty years, was no coward and

99

no fool. To outwit him, to entrap him into a damaging admission, was not going to be simple and Garnet, it could be assumed, would know exactly what evidence they wanted to hear from him. It was not a question of making him tell a lie but of persuading him to reveal a truth which might be capable of subsequent exaggeration. For what, after all, must the truth be? Garnet had been living among these traitors, seeing their covert activity, hearing their confessions, talking to their wives and having contact with their servants. Could they really have planned a revolt without his knowledge? He *must* have known about it or else (which is the same thing) he must have decided not to know about it. In Garnet the Earl of Salisbury knew that he had an opponent worthy of his steel.

In the act of interrogation it is axiomatic that the person being questioned should be confronted with alternating personalities, one or more being kind and sympathetic and at least one other being harsh and cruel. Bullied by B, the victim will then (perhaps) confide in A. In this instance the softening process began soon after Garnet's capture.

At Worcester there began between Garnet and Bromley [the Sheriff] a friendship that illustrates the quiet fascination Garnet exercised over others and had gained him friends in Rome and over all England ... Later Bromley asked Garnet and Oldcorne to be his private guests and prisoners in Holt Castle and sent his coach to bring them there. 'We were exceedingly well used,' says Garnet, 'and dined and supped with him and his every day.'[1]

When the journey began to London, he was given the best horse and was rested on the way. 'All the way to London,' as he gladly admitted, 'I was passing well used at the King's charge and that by express order from Lord Salisbury.'[2]

We need not question that the orders from Lord Salisbury were precise. Garnet and Oldcorne were taken to the Gatehouse Prison on their arrival in London on 13 February. At the Council table were Lord Salisbury, Sir John Popham, Sir Edward Coke, Sir William Wade and the Earls of Nottingham, Worcester and Northampton. Garnet had gone from school at Winchester to be a proof-reader for Richard Tottel, the well-known printer and law publisher, and had then met with John Popham, Attorney-at-law. He was now to meet him again, a man more feared even than Sir William Wade.

The Councillors treated Garnet with a great show of respect; in fact, the first interview opened with punctilious courtesy on both sides. 'When I came to the Council, I kneeled and I was bid stand,' wrote Garnet. Gerard adds: 'The Lords themselves would seldom speak unto him but they would put off their hat and sometimes hold it off for a good while'; before asking him any question, they addressed him as Mr. Garnet. One piece of abuse Salisbury, however, could not resist. He had intercepted a letter from 'Mrs. Vaux to me, subscribed, "Your loving sister, A.G."' My Lord Salisbury said 'What, you are married to Mrs. Vaux. She calls herself Garnet.' What, Senex fornicarius (old fornicator). At the next interview, however, Salisbury asked Garnet's forgiveness 'and said he spoke to me in jest'. He put his arm round Garnet's shoulders and held it there a long time. The other Councillors said that I was held for exemplar in those matters.'[3]

The questions were at first formal and then explanatory, the jibe about Mrs Vaux intended merely to test a reaction. The question about his complicity in the Gunpowder Plot was asked but then apparently forgotten. On the Council table lay a copy of Garnet's unpublished treatise on equivocation (a copy found in Tresham's room) and Salisbury turned to this, saying 'This is the high point in which you must satisfy the King, that he may know what to trust unto.' Three hours were now spent in theological discussion, the tone being still studiously polite.

Equivocation is the ambiguous use of words so as to conceal the truth without a direct lie. To equivocate is also to prevaricate, quibble or falter in what has been called a Jesuitical manner. As a hunted group of men, liable to betrayal and arrest at any time, the Jesuits in Protestant countries had acquired the characteristics of any other secret society. They had to be expert in concealing their plans and careful to protect their friends. When asked whether members of the Church of England were (in his view) heretics, Garnet thus replied that their doctrines were heretical but as to whether any individual was a heretic he did not profess to know. It was a theologically sound reply but it would pass with a hostile public as an evasion. The object of this line of questioning was to discredit his evidence in advance and there is reason to suppose that it served its purpose. The porter in *Macbeth* is made to say:

Knock, knock! Who's there, i th'other devil's name? Faith, here's an equivocator that could swear in both the scales against either scale; who committed treason enough for God's sake, yet could not equivocate to heaven: O, come in, equivocator.   *Macbeth* (Act III Scene 3)

What to a modern audience may seem a little tedious was screamingly funny when written. All London knew about equivocation before Garnet's trial was over, but Salisbury had made Garnet known as an equivocator before the trial had well begun.

On the following day, the 14th, Garnet was taken to the Tower of London, where he was given a relatively comfortable room and where his friends were allowed to provide him with a bed, chairs, bedding, coal, fruit and wine. Garnet observed (perhaps with surprise) that 'I am allowed with every meal a good draught of excellent claret wine.' Wade was hoping to entrap him in a convivial atmosphere and had evidently sensed that wine was his weakness (as, in a moderate way, it may have been). The examination continued but 'the friendliness of his examiners did not deceive him'. Neither did it extract any useful confession. Salisbury's part was now finished and he turned the case over to Popham and Coke.

The tone of the examination now changed completely. The Chief Justice and the Attorney-General, hitherto polite, were now openly hostile. Their manner contrasted with that of Carey, the jailer, who became very friendly indeed and showed an inclination towards Catholicism. His first kindness was in taking Garnet's letters into and out of the Tower. These were, of course, copied, the forgeries being delivered and the originals going to the Attorney-General. The letters were found to have some words added, written in lemon or orange juice, but were unhelpful to the prosecution. So Carey now told Garnet that Father Oldcorne had been placed in an adjacent cell and that there was a hole in the wall through which the two priests could converse. So there was but it was so arranged that their words could also be heard by two eavesdroppers posted there for the purpose. The first conversations took place on 23 February but were not especially interesting. Each heard the other's confession and each told the other what news he had heard. Another conversation, on 25 February, was equally disappointing. Only on one occasion did Garnet make a mistake but it was crucial.

... Amongst other things, Father Oldcorne demanding of Father Garnet whether Mr. Winter's going into Spain and his negotiation there were not laid to his charge, to this the Father answered, He could answer that well enough, for after that he had the King's general pardon at the time of his coming to the Crown, that other business with Spain being in the reign of Queen Elizabeth. Then Father Oldcorne also demanded whether he were not pressed with this matter of the Powder Treason, as being a likely thing they would urge that above all other matters against him. Father Garnet answered, that so they did; but that they could prove no such matter against him, and that no man living could touch him in that matter, but one.[4]

'But one' — he had given himself away with those last two words. His defences had been breached at last. It remained to make him reveal the name of that one witness. Two different tactics were now employed. He was first deprived of sleep for five nights and then given a lot of wine, possibly drugged. These tactics failed so then the order was given for the torture to be applied to him. He went to the rack and was asked again about his involvement in the plot. He denied having any part in it but admitted to 'a simple knowledge' of it, and that also in so secret a manner as that it was never lawful for him to utter it, being in confession.' He could utter it now because he had the penitent's permission. He had heard about the plot from Father Oswald Tesimond, who had it in confession from Catesby himself. Here was proved the fact of misprision of treason. Garnet had known about the plot and had not reported it to the officers of the law.

In a letter written by Salisbury on the following day the government policy is clearly laid down.

Whether Garnet lives or dies is a small matter, the important thing is to demonstrate the iniquity of the Catholics, and to prove to all the world that it is not for religion, but for their treasonable teaching and practices, that they should be exterminated. It is expedient to make manifest to the world how far these men's doctrinal practice reacheth into the bowels of treason, and so, for ever after, stop the mouths of their calumniation that preach and print of conscience.[5]

The proceedings were a public relations exercise to show that the fault of the Catholics was not merely in religious belief but in supporting doctrines which were treasonable in themselves. That Garnet knew about the plot was now proved. He could argue, however, that what was learnt in confession could not be divulged. What weakened his position was the fact that Catesby offered to tell him about the plot out of confession but that Garnet refused to listen. Had he done so he would have been in a different position but the fact remains that he preferred to be technically ignorant about a planned crime – and an appalling crime – of which he had knowledge through confession. Hoping for more damning evidence, the Council went on to have Oldcorne tortured and applied the same treatment to his servant Ralph and to John Grissold, who kept house for Anne Vaux. No further information was gained this way, nor from Garnet himself, anxious as he was to save his friends from the rack. Anne Vaux herself was brought before the Council but stood up to questioning and there was nothing, indeed, which she could have revealed. Garnet was himself examined again on 12 and 14 March, and there followed a curious episode when the questions put to Garnet came from the king himself; questions, mainly theological, which had no bearing on the case. The examinations dragged to an end and the trial was fixed for Friday, 28 March and would take place in Guildhall.

Was Garnet guilty? On this subject Professor G.M. Trevelyan argues that Greenway, first Jesuit to learn the details of the plot, probably encouraged it:

... But Garnet himself adopted a middle course. Even according to his own account, he made but feeble protestation when Catesby informed him that some violence was intended, and when he learnt the whole terrible truth from Greenway he made no serious efforts to dissuade his friends, avoided their company, gradually retired from the neighbourhood of London as the fatal autumn session drew near, and during the week when he knew the matter was to be put to the touch, lay concealed in a remote manor house on the borders of Worcestershire. Thus the Provincial of the English Jesuits acted like a coward. Either he half-approved of the design, or else the prospect of withstanding Catesby to the face terrified from his duty the one man who could successfully have forbidden the conspirators to proceed.[6]

Others might hesitate to use the word 'coward' in this context. Garnet had remained faithful to his charge, serving his cause and avoiding capture for twenty years, aware all the time that death on the scaffold would be the penalty for the slightest mistake. He left the London area for good reason – his haunts there had been discovered. About that there is no mystery. Our difficulty in understanding Garnet's position is the result of our living in a different age. We realize, in theory, that his was a very strict belief. As he himself put it, 'whatsoever is held contrary to the Church of Rome is heretical'. He also lived under a very strict discipline, taking his orders from the Society of Jesus. For those who engage in a campaign similar to his, a subversive attack on a fairly established regime, discipline is vital not merely to achieve success but even merely to survive. The underlying doctrine must be detailed and precise. There must be no splinter group or minority viewpoints. Orders must be obeyed without question. Communists today work in the same way and obey the same sort of rules. Given the situation in which a mad Marxist is about to trigger off a nuclear device that will destroy a continent and endanger the planet, a more junior comrade may refuse to intervene. 'He is my superior' the junior might explain, 'and paragraph 372 in the Big Red Book gives him the power to act.' Understanding this argument, the rest of us, not sharing his faith, would protest that there must be room in the world for common sense. Rules cannot be as sacred as that. In the last resort, we must do the sensible thing. To this the Communist or Catholic will retort 'And who are you to decide what the sensible thing is?' This is not a debate in which either side is likely to convince the other. The situation is beyond argument and we have to do something. In the argument between Garnet and Sir Edward Coke, the Jesuit was charged with having inspired the plot. He could deny this and he did. What he could not deny was that his teaching made the king a heretic to whom no true Catholic need owe allegiance. If he had not directly inspired the plot, he had been aware of it and had done nothing to prevent it. Here his defence was that he had no knowledge of the plot save through confession and that, by the rules of his Church, knowledge so acquired could not be used. We today would reply, as in the other case, that there must be room in the world for common sense. The rule in the book is not real in the sense that the gunpowder is real. The situation was beyond argument, we should agree, and Garnet had to do something but preferred, in effect, to do nothing. In the seventeenth century all controversy took a rather theological form but the attitude of the Protestant public was basically the same as ours. In the end, the individual must use his common sense.

So all the interrogation had served its end. It had shown that Garnet was an accessory to the intended crime. This was not enough, however, for the government's purpose. Garnet had been brought to London on 11 February and the trial was fixed for 28 March. All or most of the intervening period had been spent in examining Garnet on twenty-three occasions and also examining his associates, as everyone knew. To have indicted him then as a papist priest who had been ordained overseas and returned to England (itself a capital offence) would have been to admit defeat, for this basic fact was known on 11 February and was never denied by the man they sought to convict. The Attorney-General ruled out this indictment and it was generally known that he had done so. Since Garnet's admission that he knew about the plot, he was open to an indictment of misprision of treason but this again was not enough. Salisbury wanted a trial which would convict all Jesuits and all active Catholics of treason itself. In Salisbury's own words, 'It is the cause, not the person . . . We are now therefore not to arraign Garnet the Jesuit . . . but to unmask and arraign that misnamed presumptuous Society of Our Saviour Jesus . . .' He wanted to show that their teaching led logically to treason and that all were involved to that extent in the Gunpowder Plot. It had to be a Jesuit plot and Garnet had to be seen as one of the plotters and indeed as the leader of them, the instigator of the rest. This was the Attorney-General's task and it was not going to be easy. For one thing it was not true. For another, it was not even probable. As against that, the dice in a treason trial were loaded against the prisoner. He was allowed no counsel and could call no evidence. He had, it is true, a right of reply but Garnet was weakened and tired by now, wanting to have the trial over and done with. There is much that can be said against Salisbury and his colleagues, as much again against the Attorney-General and something against the king himself. What must be said for them is that they worked on the case and had reasons of state for wanting it to end in a certain way. As for Sir Edward Coke, a big, coarse and ugly man, a critic who complains of his distorting the evidence gives him credit at least for 'brilliant invective and consummate eloquence'. The trial of Garnet was to represent his masterpiece as a barrister, the climax of his career in advocacy, for he became Chief Justice of Common Pleas in 1606. For the Earl of Salisbury the trial was to represent the climax of his career in politics. In so far as his aim was to create and sustain a permanently Protestant Britain, his first step was to secure the accession of James 1, his second to discredit and weaken the Catholic opposition. The Gunpowder Plot was the 'neat device' which made that second step possible. He did not invent the plot. He watched it, rather, and may well have assisted in its development; and when the moment of discovery came, it cannot be denied that he made the best possible use of it. In the art of judo the skill of the wrestler is in using his opponent's strength to defeat itself. This was an art in which the Earl of Salisbury was supremely skilled; an art in which his touch was masterly.

9

Guildhall

Trial of Henry Garnet, Superior of the Jesuits in England, for High Treason, on Friday, the 28th day of March, 3 Jac. I, 1606 at the Guildhall of the City of London.

The trial was authorized by a special commission, issued into London, and directed to the following Commissioners:

Sir Leonard Halliday, Lord Mayor of London.
Charles Howard, Earl of Nottingham, Lord High Admiral.
Thomas Howard, Earl of Suffolk, Steward of the Household.
Edward, Earl of Worcester, Master of the Horse.
Henry Howard, Earl of Northampton, Warden of the Cinque Ports.
Robert Cecil, Earl of Salisbury, Principal Secretary of State.
Sir John Popham, Lord Chief Justice of England.
Sir Thomas Fleming, Knt, Lord Chief Baron of the Exchequer.
Sir Christopher Yelverton, Knt, one of the Judges of the King's Bench.
and several Aldermen of the City of London.

The king was present at the trial privately, with a vast assemblage of courtiers. Several foreign ambassadors also witnessed the trial, and many ladies, amongst whom were the Lady Arabella, the Countess of Suffolk, Lady Walsingham, and the Lady of Sir James Hayes, with many more. The trial lasted from eight o'clock in the morning till seven at night.

The indictment firmly accused Henry Garnet of conspiring with others to kill the king and his son, to raise sedition and rebellion, to subvert the government and the Church and to procure foreigners to invade the realm. A jury was sworn, comprising some of the wealthiest merchants in London, three of them knighted and to one of whom the king, Nottingham and Suffolk owed large sums of money. Then the Attorney-General began what was to prove a very long speech. He began with a long historical introduction going back to events of the previous reign and to the first coming of the Jesuits and to Garnet's arrival in England in 1586.

And it may here be noted, that since the Jesuits set foot in this land there never passed four years without a most pestilent and pernicious treason, tending to the subversion of the whole.[1]

All this had nothing to do with the case before the court but was background material, creating a general prejudice against the Jesuits.

In March, 1603, Garnet and Catesby, (a pestilent traitor) confer together . . . Now, without question, Catesby at this time discovered the whole plot to Garnet . . . (who approved it) . . . In June following (1604) doth Greenway, the Jesuit consult with Garnet, his Superior, about divers treasonable matter, and in such conference informs him of the whole course of the Powder Treason at large . . . In October doth Garnet meet the other traitors at Coughton, in Warwickshire . . . [The plot was openly encouraged by Greenway and Old-corne, Jesuits. All Jesuits are masters of equivocation. Greenway knew of the plot from Catesby etc. etc. etc.][2]

It was a good speech, considered as an attack on the Jesuits, and tended to convict some of them – who were not, however, on trial. What it failed to show, except by mere assertion, was that Garnet had encouraged the plot.

Garnet now had his chance to reply and he did so at length, dealing at first with the doctrine of equivocation, which he explained at some length.

Here my Lord Salisbury interrupted the prisoner and said, that because the truth was oftentimes more plainly discovered by interposition of questions and answers, than by a continual speech delivered together, he would ask of Mr.

Garnett one question concerning that doctrine he delivered. 'For you teach it,' said he, 'to be unlawful to equivocate before a competent judge, and I trust you take us to be such. At the least I do. Now did you not deny in the Tower unto me with earnest asseveration, that you had not any conference with Hall, until the witness was produced against you, and then you confessed it? Is not this to equivocate before a competent judge, and in a matter of no small consequence?' To this the prisoner answered that he did so because, until the witness came, he did think the matter wholly secret, and therefore not liable to the examination of any judge, though otherwise competent; besides he deemed it prejudicial to a third person [i.e. Carey, the jailer] whom then he accounted an honest man.[2]

Garnet went on to deal with the doctrine by which the pope could depose and excommunicate a king. Again, the Earl of Salisbury interrupted his explanation with a question: Could the pope excommunicate King James? To this Garnet replied: 'My Lord, I cannot deny the authority of His Holiness.' Garnet now went on to deal with recusants and Jesuits, coming finally to his own case. He denied having anything to do with the Gunpowder Plot. He always abhorred this wicked attempt and did all he could to prevent it. Here the Earl of Salisbury reminded him that his chief effort to prevent it had been Sir Edmond Baynham's mission to Rome, supposed to procure a prohibition of all conspiracies:

... and yet you know that Baynham was sent at such a time that he was only at Florence in October; and do you not think he had need to be well horsed to go from thence to Rome, get a prohibition, and return to England before the 5th of November?[4]

In a subsequent interchange with the Earl of Salisbury, Garnet admitted that Greenway had told him about the plot as he himself had it from Catesby. He could tell no one else because he had learnt it in confession. Then Salisbury asked leave to address the court, saying:

I hold myself greatly honoured to be an assistant amongst so many great Lords at the seat of justice, where God's cause should receive so much honour, by discrediting, in the person of Garnet, the religion of the Jesuits; and lamentable indeed it is that treason, and especially such a crime as the Powder Treason should be maintained and sheltered under the cloak of religion ...

All your defence, Mr. Garnet, is but simple negation; your negatives compared with your affirmations are merely contradictory; and your privity and activity laid together approve you manifestly guilty. I pray you, what encouraged Catesby to proceed, but your resolving him in the first proposition? What warranted Fawkes, but Catesby's application of your argument?[5]

A little later Garnet denied again that he was a party to the plot:

Earl of Salisbury: 'Mr Garnet, give me but one argument that you were not consenting to it, that can hold in any indifferent man's ear or sense, beside your bare negative.'
Whereat Garnet was mute (and possibly exhausted).
The Earl of Nottingham: 'Mr Garnet, if a man should tell you in confession that he would stab the King with a dagger tomorrow, are you not bound to reveal it?'
Mr Garnet: 'My Lord, unless I could know it by some other means I might not.'[6]
Hereupon the people fell into a great laughter . . .

The Earl of Salisbury pressed Garnet to explain why he refused to hear about the plot from Catesby.

Mr Garnet: 'I did what I could to dissuade it, and went into Warwickshire with a purpose to dissuade Mr Catesby when he should have come down . . .'
Earl of Salisbury: 'Your first answer is more absurd, seeing you knew Catesby would not come down till the 6th of November, which was the day after the blow should have been given, and you went into the country ten days before . . .'
Mr Garnet: 'My Lord, I would to God I had never known of the Powder Treason.'[6]

The trial dragged on and a number of documents were read and then, finally, the Earl of Salisbury asked the accused whether he had anything more to say:

Earl of Salisbury: 'Mr Garnet, if you have not yet done, I would have you to understand that the King hath commanded, that whatsoever, made for you, or against you, all should be read; and so it is; and we will take of you what you will. Therefore, good Mr Garnet, whatever you have to say, say on, in God's name, and you shall be heard.'[6]

Then Garnet desired the jury that they would allow of and believe those things that he had desired and affirmed; and not to give credit unto those things whereof there was no direct proof against him, nor to condemn him by any circumstance and presumptions.

> *Earl of Salisbury:* 'Mr Garnet, is this all you have to say? If it be not, take your time, no man shall interrupt you.'
> *Garnet:* 'Yea, my Lord.'[6]

The trial was over and the jury, returning after a quarter of an hour, brought in a verdict of guilty. The Lord Chief Justice then gave judgment that Garnet should be hanged, drawn and quartered.

My Lord of Salisbury again demanded if Garnet would say anything else.

> *Garnet:* 'No, my Lord; but I humbly desire your Lordships all to commend my life to the King's Majesty, nevertheless. At his pleasure I shall be ready, either to die, or to live and do him service.'[6]
> And so the Court rose.

Considering this trial, as reported, we may conclude that the prosecution could claim a measure of success. By spending time on equivocation they managed to show that Garnet was a liar. Asked whether he had been in contact with Father Oldcorne he denied it. Confronted with the evidence of their conversation, he admitted it, explaining that he was under no obligation to accuse himself. This weakened his case when he denied any prior knowledge of the plot except in confession. Given his close association with the conspirators, the fact of which had been established, it was difficult to believe that he knew nothing about it, impossible to believe that he could not have found out about it had he really wanted to know. There is only a small difference, at best, between knowing and deciding not to know. On this topic the prosecution made out a strong case and it justified the verdict of guilty. But the Attorney-General was far less successful in proving that Garnet and Catesby had planned the conspiracy together or even that Garnet had been given full details in March 1603. To have proved him a liar in another context did admittedly weaken the effect of his denials. As against that, the plot ran counter to papal and Jesuit policy and could not have been welcome to Garnet. There is little reason to suppose that its success would have placed a Catholic monarch on the throne. The effect, on the other hand, of its far more probable failure was disastrous from the Catholic point of view. Aware of this weakness in his case, Sir Edward Coke went back over history to show that plotting is a Jesuit habit and that the existence of a plot allows us to assume that there must be a Jesuit at the bottom of it. To the one man in the dock he added a crowd of other traitors chosen from history and tried to indict them as a whole. This was effective as propaganda but should have been inadmissible in law. The guilt of other Jesuits, proven or not, was irrelevant to the case before the court and so was the fact that the pope claimed the right to depose King James I. But the trial of Garnet was not an ordinary trial nor was its outcome a matter merely of life or death. 'It is expedient', as Salisbury said, 'to make manifest to the world how far these men's doctrinal practices reacheth into the bowels of treason.' By the end of the trial this point had been fairly made.

That is not to say that the Council was completely satisfied with the trial and verdict. The Attorney-General and others hoped, therefore, that Garnet would make a more complete confession after sentence had been pronounced. After his condemnation to death he had no motive, they argued, for further equivocation. So there were days of further examination between the sentence and its execution. It cannot be said that these efforts served any purpose. Garnet was prevailed upon to make various statements but they add nothing to our knowledge of the plot. In one of these he emphasized his disapproval of the conspiracy and added:

. . I acknowledge that I was bound to reveal all knowledge that I had of this or any other treason out of the sacrament of confession. And whereas, partly upon hope of prevention, partly for that I would not betray my friend, I did not reveal the general knowledge of Mr Catesby's intentions which I had by him, I do acknowledge myself highly guilty, to have offended God, the King's majesty and estate; and humbly ask of all forgiveness; exhorting all Catholics whatsoever, that they no way build upon my example, but by prayer and otherwise seek the peace of the realm . . .[7]

After all the questions were over, the day of execution was fixed as 3 May and the place was to be St Paul's Churchyard, 'over against the Bishop's house'.

... In that place there was a great scaffold made, and a gibbet in the midst of the scaffold. And such multitude of people, noble and ignoble, so many standings set up by carpenters to hire out for money, that a mere place to stand on would cost twelvepence well; and the party from whom I chiefly have many of these particulars ... was glad to give twelvepence only to stand upon a wall. All windows were full, yea, the tops of the houses full of people, so that it is not known the like hath been at any execution.[8]

Garnet was drawn on a hurdle from the Tower and was met near the scaffold by the Recorder of London (Sir Henry Montague), the Dean of St Paul's and the Dean of Winchester. The Dean of St Paul's said, 'Mr Garnet, I am sent unto you from His Majesty, to will you, that now being in the last hour of your mortal life, you will perform the duty of a true subject to which you are obliged by the laws of God and nature; and therefore to disclose such treason as you know intended towards His Majesty's danger and the Commonwealth.' To this Father Garnet answered, 'Mr Dean, it may please you to tell His Majesty, that I have been arraigned, and what could be laid to my charge, I have there answered, and said as much as I could; so that in this place I have no more to say.' One would have thought that these last interrogations might have left it at that but Garnet was now urged to address the people. His voice was too weak to be heard at any distance but the Recorder repeated his words loudly as he avowed his disapproval of the plot. Prompted again, he asked the king's pardon for not revealing what he knew of the plot from Mr Catesby – but not otherwise. The Dean of Winchester then told him that he, Garnet, had been privy to the whole business. A long argument followed in the course of which the Recorder urged him not to extenuate his crime by cunning and duplicity. Garnet sensibly refused to be drawn into another debate about equivocation but said that he was thought to be more guilty than he really was, as he was not the author or contriver of the plot. He finally climbed the ladder, said his prayers and then the ladder was removed. By the express command of the king, he remained hanging from the gallows until he was quite dead. So died Henry Garnet, the Jesuit, not the wisest nor the saintliest of men but well-meaning, pious and brave, well loved by many Catholics and since widely regarded as a martyr for his faith. As the Earl of Salisbury so properly said, 'Whether Garnet lives or dies is a small matter.' What his death was to prove was that the English Catholics were guilty not of Catholicism but of treason. What further proof could any honest man require?

10

Aftermath

THE Gunpowder Plot gave rise to a copious literature at the time, headed by *A Discourse of the manner of the Discovery of the Gunpowder Plot*, published by the King's Printer, probably written by Francis Bacon but popularly ascribed (with official encouragement) to the king himself. This was printed before the trials took place and was followed by an official account of the trials themselves. With these there appeared many ephemeral works in which 'The Devil of the Vault' appeared as a central character. Many of them were illustrated with woodcuts in which Guy Fawkes is shown, lantern in hand, at the moment of his arrest. On these numerous prints the comment has been made that:

In no single instance is Guy Fawkes represented as about to blow up the right house. Sometimes it is the House of Commons that he is going to destroy, more frequently the Painted Chamber, often a nondescript building corresponding to nothing in particular – but in no single instance is it the House of Lords.[1]

This literature and these illustrations (however misleading) served to perpetuate the memory of the plot. Verses set to music served the same purpose even more effectively and one of them voiced the sentiment:

> I see no reason
> Why gunpowder treason
> Should ever be forgot.

That it should be remembered was government policy and the celebration of the anniversary was decided from the outset, replacing the king's previous observance relating to the Gowrie Conspiracy. That bonfires should mark the occasion was inevitable and that Guy Fawkes should be burnt in effigy was obviously appropriate.

The name Guy, thus immortalized, was not a common name in England but was the name given to Sir Guy Fairfax, member of Gray's Inn, Recorder of York (1476), Judge of the King's Bench and Chief Justice of the Duchy of Lancaster (died 1495). The Fairfaxes were and are a Yorkshire family and the name Guy remained in that family and was copied by neighbours in the vicinity of York. From that small beginning the name Guy attached itself to the effigy destined for the bonfire and so to any man whose face could be said to resemble a crudely made figure. In English usage it became possible to describe someone as 'a regular guy'; a stuffed dummy in other words, and a figure of fun. Moving to the new world, the word 'guy' was extended to any and every man and came to be used even in commendation, as in saying that some man 'is quite a guy'. In its more extended application a guy is thus no more and no less than a man, contrasted latterly with a doll, who is no more and no less than a woman. In this surprising way the name Guy has come to have a wider circulation than any other name, used frequently throughout North America and known throughout the world through repetition in motion-picture dialogue.

This was one short-term and long-term sequel to the Gunpowder Plot. Another short-term sequel was an even stricter legislation against the Catholics in England. Under a new Act James I required all Catholics to take a new oath of supremacy, renouncing the doctrine that the pope could depose kings. The pope decreed that Catholics must refuse to take the oath, making them choose in effect between disloyalty and heresy. In practice Blackwell, the Archpriest, allowed Catholics to take the oath, those that did so being actually, though not legally, exempt from the recusant fines. The more pious, who followed the pope's ruling, were subject to continued persecution until 1619, the period of the proposed Spanish match. Later in the century there was more intense persecution at the time of the Popish Plot of 1678 and a renewed interest in the Gunpowder Plot itself. A result of this interest was a new book on the subject, written by Dr Thomas Barlow, Bishop of Lincoln, and refuting 'a bold and groundless surmise that all this was a contrivance of Secretary Cecil'. Some revived interest in this subject led the government of the day to ask whether the risk was merely historical. The cellars beneath the Parliament building had been leased out to private persons during the intervening years but it was now decided that this practice should cease. It was resolved

that all timber, fire-wood, coals and other materials, of what kind soever, be removed out of the said cellars and vaults and that passages be forthwith made through all the said cellars and vaults, to the end that soldiers and sentinels, with trusty officers over them, may continually, night and day, walk to and fro, and watch in the said cellars and vaults, till further order.[2]

This precaution has since been discontinued. It was also thought appropriate that the cellars should more especially be searched on the eve of each Parliament state opening. The first search was carried out in 1678 by Sir Christopher Wren and Sir James Moore and the custom has been observed from that day to this.

These are reminders of the Gunpowder Plot but the more immediate result, following hard on the trial and execution of Henry Garnet, was the Earl of Salisbury's admission to the Order of the Garter. This honour was not unusual for a nobleman who held such high office but a special significance surrounded the occasion. He was, beyond question, the hero of the hour, and this period represents the height of his political career. He was losing favour by 1612 and would have been out of office had he lived any longer. But for him, however, it was felt at the time, the plot might have succeeded. The time had come to do him honour and it was done with all appropriate pomp and circumstance. Catholicism had been defeated and discredited, the power of the old nobility had been checked, and the way had been prepared for the eventual union of England and Scotland, a union only possible between two permanently Protestant countries. The earldom to which he had already been raised was at this time the highest rank of the English nobility. The arrival of Dukes from Scotland was to change this, leading to the revival of this rank in England, but an earldom was still the height of ambition in 1606 with only the Garter as a final ornament.

We have it on Selden's authority that the Most Noble Order of the Garter 'exceeds in majesty, honour and fame all chivalrous fraternities in the world'. If it did so in his day (and still more in ours) it is partly because its origin is at once ancient and obscure. The Knights are held to be the successors of those earlier knights who met round King Arthur's Round Table, and it would be difficult indeed to prove that they are not. If we accepted King Arthur as the founder, however, we have to concede that the Garter itself, the specific insignia, was first adopted by King Edward III and perhaps in August 1348. As from an early date the Order has been closely associated with Saint George, England's patron saint, and its traditional day of meeting has always been St George's Day. The sovereign is head of the Order, his principal officers being the Prelate, the Chancellor, the Registrar (the Dean of Windsor), Garter Principal King of Arms and the Usher of the Black Rod. By tradition the Knights number twenty-four, each having his stall in St George's Chapel in Windsor. During the reign of King James I the Knights elected were so far:

Henry Frederick, Prince of Wales
Christian IV, King of Denmark
Lodowick Stuart, Duke of Richmond and Lenox
Henry Wriothesley, Earl of Southampton
John Erskine, Earl of Mar
William Herbert, Earl of Pembroke
Ulrick, Duke of Holstein.
Robert Cecil, Earl of Salisbury, was to come next, being followed by:
Thomas Howard, Viscount Bindon
George Hume, Earl of Dunbar
Philip Herbert, Earl of Pembroke and Montgomery
Charles Stuart, Duke of York

Other and later knights were to include Frederick v, King of Bohemia, Maurice of Nassau, Prince of Orange, Christian II, Duke of Brunswick and Gustavus Adolphus, King of Sweden. It will be clear from the list of names that the Order was fairly exclusive and that election to it was, as it still is, an honour reserved for the few and one which depends, incidentally, on the occurrence of a vacancy. At about the time of the Gunpowder Plot there were, in fact, two vacancies – one caused by the death of George Clifford, Earl of Cumberland and the other caused by the death of Charles Blount, Earl of Devonshire. Rumours about how the vacancies were to be filled were recorded by the Venetian ambassador in a letter to his government:

> Yesterday was St. George's Day and the solemn ceremony of that Order was celebrated. Some of the Ambassadors were present. The King intended to raise the number of the Knights to the full twenty-four by the creation of the Earl of Salisbury and the Earl of Montgomery, his great favourites; but nothing has been done, owing, they say, to the complaints of the King of France and Denmark, Knights of the Order, who have declared that, unless the Order is kept pure by the election of those only whose nobility of blood and rank are eminent, they will resign.[3]

These rumours had little substance, for the election of the Earl of Salisbury took place almost immediately, together with that of Thomas Howard, Viscount Bindon. By the Statutes of the Order every Knight Elect is within a year after his Election to be ready to proceed to his Installation in St George's Chapel. Robert Cecil and Thomas Howard did not delay over it but were installed, in fact, on 20 May 1606. Here again we are indebted to the Venetian ambassador, who was greatly impressed:

> *May* 31
> A few days ago the Earl of Salisbury and the other new knight went to Windsor for the solemn reception of the investiture of the Garter. The pomp was such that the like of it is not in the memory of man; indeed all confess that it surpassed the ceremony of the very King's Coronation . . . All envy of him (Salisbury) is now dead; no one seeks ought but to win his favour; it is thought that his power will last for it is based not so much on the grace of his

Majesty's as on an excellent prudence and ability which secure for him the universal opinion that he is worthy of his great authority and good fortune.[4]

As the occasion was one of such exceptional splendour it is surprising that we know so little about it. In the description which follows we rely mostly on general accounts of seventeenth-century Installations and must assume that the Earl of Salisbury had more than his share of acclaim.

When the Garter ceremony is filmed today we are shown an event which has taken place at Windsor. In the time of Elizabeth I and James I the big crowds collected, in fact, in London. The procession started there and was thus seen by the public before the Installation took place.

In the reign of previous sovereigns it had been the custom for the knights elect to proceed from London to Windsor in grand procession in order to be installed. They took up their lodging in the Strand, in Salisbury Court, in Holborn or within the City; and thence rode on horseback to Windsor accompanied by a large party of friends and attendants. It was a dazzling sight in those days, to see the cavalcade starting from the City residence of a knight and vast were the throngs which gathered in the streets, to see the train of horsemen with their gorgeous apparel and plumes of feathers, passing along on their way to Windsor. But to such excesses of grandeur were the knights elect sometimes carried by their ambition that James I put limits to the extent of the procession, and enacted, 'that every one of the knight-companions should have fifty persons to attend him unto the annual solemnities of the order and no more'.[5]

James I is believed to have limited this display in the interests of his Scottish nobles, who lacked the means to compete, but his rule does not refer, it would seem, to the ceremony of Installation. And even were a nobleman to limit the number present of his own household, no rule could exclude his friends. The Earl of Salisbury's friends were numerous but it is a question whether anyone of consequence could be absent from the procession which attended so powerful a minister. When the Earls of Danby and Morton were installed during the reign of Charles I they made their way severally to Hyde Park:

... each having two noblemen to support him, with their footmen, in rich coats, on either side of them.

Their gentlemen ushers rode bareheaded and before them the officers of arms, wearing their coats, and their servants in blue coats and cognizances (as was the ancient mode), were led on by trumpets. The rest of the lords, knights and gentlemen followed after each knight elect's troop, according to their rank and quality foremost. The proceeding of the Earl of Morton was marshalled in this manner:

Trumpets, two and two,

Grooms, in coats, two and two

Yeomen, two and two

Gentlemen, two and two

Secretaries

Stewards

Gentlemen of the Horse

Pages

Four Officers of Arms

Gentleman Usher, bare

Lancaster Herald, covered

Earl Morton, supported

between two chief lords

Footmen on each side in

rich coats

Noblemen and Gentlemen

according to their degrees[6]

We may assume that the Earl of Salisbury was at least as well attended. But did he really ride from London to Windsor? The likelihood is, surely, that he rode out of London, rode into Windsor, and went the rest of the way by coach. It would seem that all order was usually lost on the way and that the procession had always to re-form at Slough. After a ceremonial entry to the Castle, the Knights Elect were conducted to their several apartments.

For an elderly statesman even the ceremony itself must be an ordeal. It reached, and reaches, a climax at two moments; the putting on of the garter and of the surcoat. For the former part of the ritual the accompanying words read as follows:

122

INVESTITURE

The Loving Company of the Order of the Garter hath received you their Brother and Fellow, and in token of this, they give and present you this present Garter, which God grant that you receive and wear from henceforth to his Praise and Glory, and to the Exaltation and Honour of the said Noble Order and yourself.

When the Knight Elect receives his Surcoat, the Registrar reads these words:

Take this Robe of Crimson to the increase of your Honour and in token or sign of the most Noble Order you have received, wherewith you being defended, may be bold, not only strong to fight but also to offer yourself to shed your Blood for Christ's Faith, the Liberties of the Church and the just and necessary defence of them that are oppressed and needy.[7]

And what of the robes and insignia?

The Garter, of dark blue ribbon edged with gold, bearing the motto, 'Honi soit qui mal y pense' in gold letters with buckle and pendant of gold richly chased, is worn on the left leg below the knee.

The Mantle is of blue velvet, lined with white taffeta; on the left breast the star is embroidered.

The Hood is of crimson velvet.

The Hat is of black velvet lined with white taffeta; the plume of white ostrich feathers, in the centre of which a tuft of black heron's feathers, all fastened to the hat by a band of diamonds.

The Collar, gold, consists of twenty-six pieces, each in the form of a garter, enamelled azure and appended thereto:

The George, or figure of St. George on horseback encountering the dragon.

The George is worn to the collar, and the lesser George pendant to a dark blue ribbon over the left shoulder.

The Star, of eight points silver, has upon the centre the Cross of St. George, gules, encircled with the garter.[8]

After the ceremony, long in itself, came the banquet, which must have lasted for hours. When all was over, Robert Cecil could go at last to bed. He was Baron Cecil of Effingdon, Viscount Cranborne, Earl of Salisbury, Privy Councillor, His Majesty's Secretary of State and a future Lord High Treasurer of England. To all these honours he could now add his Knighthood of the Garter, the final proof of his success. Almost a dwarf and a hunchback from the beginning, often in poor health and deeply in debt, Robert Cecil must have felt utterly exhausted. He had worked hard for his sovereign, for his country, and these honours were the reward. His was the astute brain which had used the Gunpowder Plot to good purpose, ruining Northumberland, strengthening the Crown, discrediting the Jesuits and assisting the Protestant cause. He knew more about the plot than would ever become public for he was a secretive man and the knowledge would die with him. Did he give any further thought to those he may have encouraged, to those whose execution he had brought about? The likelihood is rather that he would soon have all but forgotten them and their plot and the manner of their death. For he had other things to think about: the daily work of administration and diplomacy, the plan for an alliance with the Dutch Republic, the possibility of mediating between France and Spain, the problems created by the king's extravagance. And beyond these affairs of state were his own affairs and finances, the building of his palaces, the planning of his gardens and the development of his estates. First there was Cranborne and then Theobalds and later, after the king had made him accept the exchange, there was Hatfield.

For garden, (speaking of those which are indeed princelike, as we have done of buildings), contents ought not well to be under thirty acres of ground; and to be divided in three parts; a green in the entrance, a heath or desert in the going forth, and the main garden in the midst; besides alleys on both sides.[9]

So his cousin, Francis Bacon, advised, and Robert Cecil may well have heeded the advice. His grounds at Hatfield would not be without fountains, statues and hedges clipped into shapes of fantasy. After he was gone and after his policies were forgotten, Hatfield would remain as his memorial; a home he had planned but would never see completed, a stately palace in an ordered setting, a quiet mansion dreaming in the sun.

Appendix 1

The Birthplace of Guy Fawkes

IT has been known since 1933 that Edward Fawkes, father of Guy, was a tenant of the Dean and Chapter of York and lived in Stonegate. Guy was baptized in the parish church of St Michael-le-Belfry and there is every reason to suppose that he was born in the parish and at his parents' house. That the house was in Stonegate is clear but it was not identified until Miss Katharine M. Longley published the results of her patient and careful research in 1973. By tracing the successive leases and collating these with a plan made in 1862, she was able to establish that the Fawkes family lived in a house, long since demolished, on the site of premises now numbered 32–34. The author is greatly indebted to Miss Longley for permission to quote from her work, first printed in *Recusant History*, January 1973. The sketch map, p. 126, based on her work, shows the relationship of the Fawkes' home to York Minster and St Michael-le-Belfry, the Church which stands between High Petergate and Minster Yard.

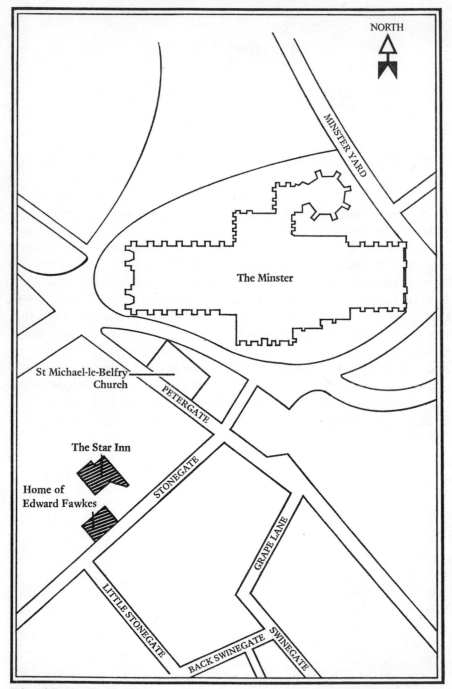

Edward Fawkes lived in the house adjacent to what is now the Star Inn. Guy Fawkes was probably born there and certainly brought up there. The site is now occupied by premises numbered 32–34 Stonegate.

Appendix II

Site of the intended explosion

PLAN one shows the general relationship of Westminster Hall (all that survives of the old Palace of Westminster); St Stephen's Chapel, the old House of Commons; White Hall and the old House of Lords. The building adjacent to the House of Lords on the south side, sometimes called the Princes Chamber, was the one under which the first cellar was hired. A lane later called Parliament Place passed this building and led to the river at Parliament Stair. The engraving (p. 129) shows the relationship of the original mine to the cellar which afterwards became available under the House of Lords itself. Illustration 26 opp. p. 53 gives a rough idea of the Palace of Westminster as a whole, contrasted with the present Palace which the older building strongly influenced in general layout. Plan two gives an approximate idea of where the explosion would have taken place, in relation to the House of Lords as it exists today.

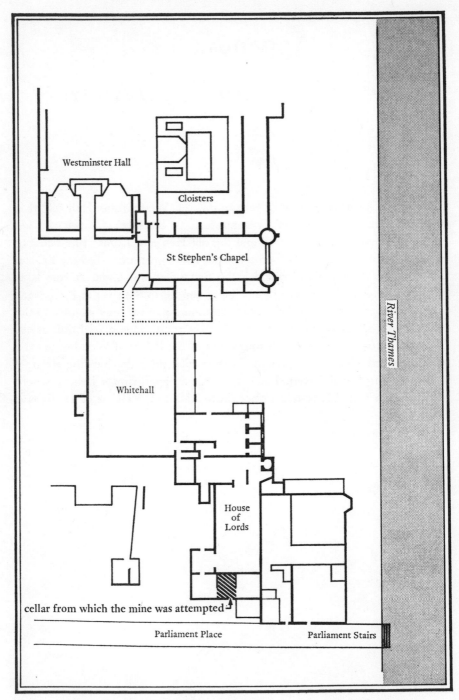

Plan one: a plan of the Houses of Parliament as they were in the seventeenth century.

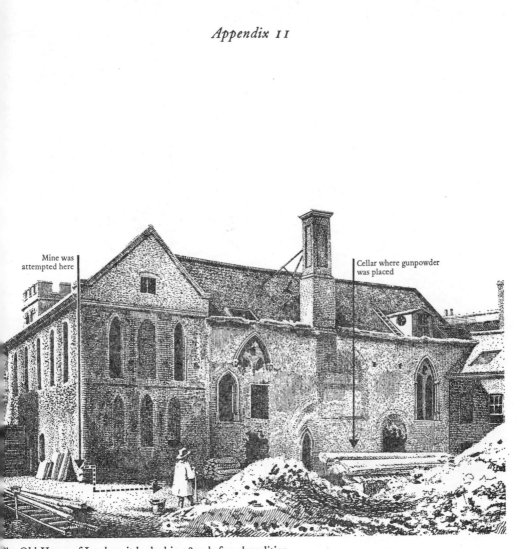

Mine was
attempted here

Cellar where gunpowder
was placed

Appendix 11

he Old House of Lords as it looked in 1809 before demolition.

129

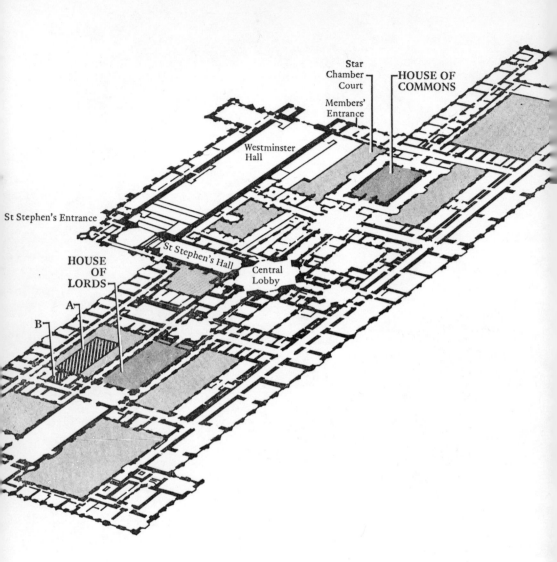

Star
Chamber
Court

Members'
Entrance

HOUSE OF
COMMONS

Westminster
Hall

St Stephen's Entrance

St Stephen's Hall

Central
Lobby

HOUSE
OF
LORDS

A

B

Plan two: The Gunpowder Plot as related to the present Houses of Parliament.
A indicates the position of the cellar from which the conspirators attempted to undermine
the House of Lords.
B indicates the position of the vault under the House of Lords itself.

Reference Notes

CHAPTER ONE

1   Norman S. Brett-Jones, *The Growth of Stuart London* (London 1935), p. 63
2   Alison Plowden, *Danger to Elizabeth: The Catholics Under Elizabeth* 1 (London 1973), p. 92
3   Plowden, *Danger to Elizabeth*, p. 235
4   *Ibid.*
5   Algernon Cecil, *A Life of Robert Cecil, First Earl of Salisbury* (London 1915), p. 374
6   G. B. Harrison, *A Jacobean Journal* (London 1941), 1 April 1603

CHAPTER TWO

1   Francis Edwards, S.J., *The Marvellous Chance* (London 1968), pp. 33–4
2   Edwards, *The Marvellous Chance*, p. 264
3   J. A. Froude, *The History of England from the Fall of Wolsey to the Defeat of the Spanish Armada* (1856–70), Vol. VI, pp. 239–53
4   J. B. Black, *The Reign of Elizabeth* (Oxford 1936), p. 371
5   Edwards, *The Marvellous Chance*, Appendix IV

CHAPTER THREE

1   David Jardine, *A Narrative of the Gunpowder Plot* (London 1837), p. 16
2   *Guy Fawkes in Spain: the 'Spanish Treason' in Spanish Documents* (London 1971), Appendix p. 62
3   A. L. Rowse, *Ralegh and the Throckmortons* (London 1962), pp. 234–6
4   Harrison, *Jac. Journ.*, 1 November 1603
5   Harrison, *Jac. Journ.*, 4 May 1603
6   H. H. Spink, *The Gunpowder Plot* (London 1902), p. 26

CHAPTER FOUR

1   G. Goodman, *The Court of King James the First* (London 1839), Vol. II,
    p. 118
2   Harrison, *Jac. Journ.*, 23 July 1604

CHAPTER FIVE

1   David Jardine, *Criminal Trials* (London 1835), Vol. II, pp. 48–9
2   Goodman, *The Court of King James* I, Vol. II, pp. 120–1
3   Philip Caraman, *Henry Garnet (1555–1606) and the Gunpowder Plot*
    (London 1964), p. 322
4   Goodman, *The Court of King James* I, Vol. I, pp. 104–5
5   David Jardine, *A Narrative of the Gun Powder Plot* (London 1857), p. 35
6   H. R. Williamson, *The Gunpowder Plot* (London 1951), p. 145
7   Spink, *The Gunpowder Plot*, pp. 9–10
8   Francis Edwards, S.J., *Guy Fawkes* (London 1969), p. 145
9   Jardine, *A Narrative of the Gun Powder Plot*, p. 100
10 Jardine, *A Narrative of the Gun Powder Plot*, p. 103

CHAPTER SIX

1   Jardine, *A Narrative of the Gunpowder Plot*, pp. 72 *et seq.*
2   Jardine, *A Narrative of the Gunpowder Plot*, p. 124
3   Jardine, *Criminal Trials*, Vol. II, p. 192
4   Caraman, *Henry Garnet*, pp. 336–7
5   Jardine, *Criminal Trials*, p. 120 (footnote)

CHAPTER SEVEN

1   Jardine, *Criminal Trials*, Vol. II, p. 129
2   Jardine, *Criminal Trials*, Vol. II, p. 130
3   Jardine, *Criminal Trials*, Vol. II, pp. 135 *et seq.*
4   Jardine, *Criminal Trials*, Vol. II, pp. 150 *et seq.*
5   Jardine, *Criminal Trials*, Vol. II, pp. 172–8
6   Jardine, *Criminal Trials*, Vol. II, pp. 160–70
7   Harrison, *Jac. Journ.*, 9 November 1605
8   Jardine, *Criminal Trials*, Vol. II, pp. 153–4
9   Harrison, *Jac. Journ.*, 6 November 1605
10 Harrison, *Jac. Journ.*, 27 June 1606
11 Jardine, *Criminal Trials*, Vol. II, pp. 124 *et seq.*

CHAPTER EIGHT

1 Caraman, *Henry Garnet*, p. 344
2 Caraman, *Henry Garnet*, pp. 321–48
3 Caraman, *Henry Garnet*, pp. 349–50
5 John Gerard, S.J., *The Condition of Catholics under James* I (London 1871), pp. 169–70
5 Caraman, *Henry Garnet*, p. 376
6 G. M. Trevelyan, *England Under the Stuarts* (Revised edition), London 1947), p. 76

CHAPTER NINE

1 Jardine, *Criminal Trials*, Vol. II, p. 248
2 Jardine, *Criminal Trials*, Vol. II, pp. 135 *et seq.*
3 Gerard, *The Condition of the Catholics under James* I, pp. 245–6
4 Jardine, *Criminal Trials*, Vol. II, pp. 135 *et seq.*
5 Jardine, *Criminal Trials*, Vol. II, pp. 295, 297
6 Jardine, *Criminal Trials*, Vol. II, pp. 135 *et seq.*
7 Jardine, *Criminal Trials*, Vol. II, p. 323
8 Gerard, *The Condition of the Catholics under James* I, p. 290

CHAPTER TEN

1 John Gerard, S.J., *What was the Gunpowder Plot?* (London 1897), p. 228
2 I. T. Smith, *Antiquities of Westminster* (London 1807), p. 43
3 *Calendar of State Papers and Manuscripts existing in the Archives and Collections of Venice*, 1603–7 (London 1900), Vol. x, p. 344
4 *Cal. of State Papers and Man. existing in the Arch. and Coll. of Venice*, p. 354
5 John Stoughton, *Notices of Windsor in the Olden Time* (Windsor 1844), p. 171
6 Stoughton, *Notices of Windsor*, p. 171
7 Joseph Pote, *The History and Antiquities of Windsor Castle* (1749), p. 219
8 Sir Bernard Burke, *The Book of Orders of Knighthood* (London 1858), p. 99
9 Peter Pauper ed., *The Essays or Counsels of Francis Bacon of Gardens*, p. 181

Index